AF560798

GREAT FINANCIAL CRISIS OF THE WORLD

GREAT FINANCIAL CRISIS OF THE WORLD

DR. RANJIT SINGH
Assistant Professor
Department of Business Administration
Assam University (A Central University)
Silchar (Assam)

and

PROF. AMALESH BHOWAL
Professor and Head
Department of Commerce
Assam University (A Central University)
Diphu Campus, Karbi Anglong (Assam)

DEEP & DEEP PUBLICATIONS PVT. LTD.
F-159, Rajouri Garden, New Delhi - 110 027

GREAT FINANCIAL CRISIS OF THE WORLD

ISBN 978-81-8450-390-6

Typeset by RAHUL COMPOSERS
358, Pocket-B, Phase-2, Sector-16B, Dwarka, New Delhi - 110 075

Printed in India at MAYUR ENTERPRISES
WZ Plot No. 3, Gujjar Market, Tihar Village, New Delhi - 110 018

Published by DEEP & DEEP PUBLICATIONS PVT. LTD.
F-159, Rajouri Garden, New Delhi - 110 027 • Phone : 25435369, 25440916
E-mail : ddpubs@gmail.com • ddpubs@yahoo.com
Showroom :
2/13, Ansari Road, Daryaganj, New Delhi - 110 002 • Telefax : 23245122

Contents

Preface

It is said that there is enough in the nature to satisfy the needs of the human being but not the greed of human being. In past, the world has faced several financial crises. If we go into the root of all these financial crises, it is seen that the root cause of all these crises are the human greed. G.B. Shaw once said that "We have learned from the history that we have learned nothing from the history and the history has the bad habit of repeating itself". Although the causes of the financial crises are the human greed, but very soon the lessons of the particular financial crisis are forgotten by the mankind and therefore, the history keeps on repeating. In the 20th century and early 21st century, the world has seen many financial crises, some of which were associated with banking panics, and many recessions coincided with these panics. There are many other situations also which are often called as financial crises. These situations include stock market crashes and the bursting of other financial bubbles like burst of dot com bubble and burst of housing bubble, etc. Currency crises and cases of sovereign defaults are also considered as the financial crisis.

Financial crisis is not very uncommon in the history. There are many financial crises the world has faced till date. The causes of financial crisis every time may not be same, but the impact of the crisis is severe all the time. So, it better to understand the nature and causes of the crisis and take lessons from them so that the same kind of mistake is not repeated in the future. This book will help the readers in understanding all these issues relating to the financial crisis.

In this book, thirteen major financial crises faced by the world starting from the great depression of 1929 to the latest sub-prime crisis are covered. The book is simply the compilation of the major incidents relating to the financial crisis and all the fact and figures are taken from the secondary sources.

Any other comments and suggestions for the improvement of the book are highly solicited.

DR. RANJIT SINGH
PROF. AMALESH BHOWAL

1 Financial Crisis—Introduction

The term *'Financial Crisis'* is referred broadly to situations in which some financial institutions or assets suddenly lose a large part of their value. In the 20th century and early 21st century, the world has seen many financial crises, some of which were associated with banking panics, and many recessions coincided with these panics. There are many other situations also which are often called as financial crises. These situations include stock market crashes and the bursting of other financial bubbles like burst of dot com bubble and burst of housing bubble, etc. Currency crises and cases of sovereign defaults are also considered as the financial crisis.

Overview of the Chapter
The Current chapter elaborates the term 'Financial Crisis' in detail. The chapter highlights the following important headings: • Types of Financial Crisis • Causes and Consequences of Financial Crisis • Theories of Financial Crisis • Different Financial Crisis in the world • Conclusion

Many economists have developed theories on financial crises explaining the caused of financial crisis and how they could be prevented.

TYPES OF FINANCIAL CRISIS

There are several types of financial crisis. The world has seen several financial crises. The nature of the entire crisis was not the same. Depending upon the nature of financial crisis, the financial crisis can be categorized into following types:

Banking Crises

There were many financial crises in the history which actually started with banking crisis. The banking crisis started with a situation called 'bank run'. The 'bank run' is referred to a situation when a bank suffers a sudden rush of withdrawals by the depositors. Since banks lend out most of the cash which they receive in deposits, it is difficult for them to quickly pay back all deposits if these are suddenly demanded. Therefore, a run may leave the bank in bankruptcy. It may result into lose of savings by many depositors unless they are covered by deposit insurance. The term 'bank run' may leads to two situations—one is *banking panic* and the other is *credit crunch.* A situation in which bank runs are widespread is called a *systemic banking crisis* or just a *banking panic.* A situation without widespread bank runs, but in which banks are reluctant to lend, because they worry that they have insufficient funds available, is often called a *credit crunch.*

Examples of bank runs include the run on the Bank of the United States in 1931 and the run on Northern Rock in 2007. The collapse of Bear Stearns in 2008 has also sometimes been called a bank run, even though Bear Stearns was an investment bank rather than a commercial bank. The U.S. savings and loan crisis of the 1980s led to a credit crunch which is seen as a major factor in the U.S. recession of 1990-91. In India, because of the strict regulatory measures there has not been any major situation of bank run. But in the early part of 21st century there are some cases registered of bank run with the Global Trust Bank.

International Financial Crises

A country may suddenly force to devalue its currency because of speculative attacks. This is to be done when a country maintains a fixed exchange rate. Sudden devaluation of the currency if not planned properly may lead to currency crisis or balance of payments crisis. In case of balance of payment crisis, the country may find it difficult to pay its sovereign debt and it may ultimately fail to pay its sovereign debt. When a country fails to pay back its sovereign debt, this is called a *sovereign default.* While devaluation and default could both be voluntary decisions of the government, they are often perceived to be the involuntary results of a change in investor sentiment that leads to a sudden stop in capital inflows into the country or a sudden increase in *capital flight* from the country.

The world has witnessed several crisis of this kind till date. Some of the crises of this kind are currency crisis of Europe when currencies that formed part of the European Exchange Rate Mechanism suffered crises in 1992-93 and were forced to devalue or withdraw from the mechanism. Another round of currency crises took place in Asia in 1997-98. Many Latin American countries defaulted on their debt in the early 1980s. The 1998 Russian financial crisis resulted in a devaluation of the ruble and default on Russian government bonds.

Speculative Bubbles and Crashes

Financial assets like stocks or bonds are called as fairly valued when their price is equal to the present value of future income from such instruments such as interest or dividends. But when the prices of these assets exceeds their fair value then in the opinions of most of the economists, these financial assets exhibits a bubble when its price exceeds the present value of the future income that would be received by owning the stock till maturity. If most market participants buy the financial asset primarily in hopes of selling it later at a higher price, instead of buying it for the income which will be generated by the asset in the future, it is evident that a bubble is present. If there is a bubble, there is also a risk of a *crash* in asset prices. Market participants will go on buying only as long as they expect that there are other participants in the market to buy the same asset. In a situation, when many market participants decide to sell the asset then the price will start to fall. However, it is difficult to tell in practice whether an asset's price actually equals its fundamental value, so it is hard to detect bubbles reliably.

There are several well-known examples of bubbles (or purported bubbles) and crashes in stock prices and other asset prices. Some of these are the Dutch tulip mania, the Wall Street Crash of 1929, the Japanese property bubble of the 1980s, the crash of the dot-com bubble in 2000-2001, and the now-deflating United States housing bubble of 2008, stock market crash of 2008 in all the major stock markets in the world.

Wider Economic Crises

When a downturn in the economic growth lasts for several quarters usually four quarters, then it is called that the economy is in recession. Technically, when an economy registered negative growth for the four consecutive quarters, the economy is said to be in recession. An especially prolonged recession may be called a *depression,* while a long period of slow but not necessarily negative growth is sometimes called *economic stagnation*. Since these phenomena affect much more than the financial system, they are not usually considered financial crises *per se*. But some economists have argued that many recessions have been caused largely because of financial crises. One important example is the Great Depression, which was preceded in many countries by bank runs and stock market crashes. The sub-prime mortgage crisis and the bursting of other real estate bubbles around the world are widely expected to lead to recession in the U.S. and a number of other countries in 2008.

Nonetheless, some economists argue that financial crises are caused by recessions instead of the other way around. Also, even if a financial crisis is the initial shock that sets-off a recession, other factors may be more important in prolonging the recession. In particular, Milton Friedman and Anna Schwartz argued that the initial economic decline associated with the crash of 1929 and the bank panics of the 1930s would not have turned into a prolonged depression if it had not been reinforced by monetary policy mistakes on the part of the Federal Reserve.

CAUSES AND CONSEQUENCES OF FINANCIAL CRISES

The cause and consequences of several financial crises are not the same. But there are some causes and certain consequences which are common in all the crises. In this section the causes and consequences of financial crisis have been discussed in detail.

Strategic Complementarities in Financial Markets

It is often observed that successful investment requires each investor in a financial market to guess what other investors will do. George Soros has called this need to guess the intentions of others 'reflexivity'. Similarly, John Maynard Keynes compared financial markets to a beauty contest game in which each participant tries to predict which model *other* participants will consider most beautiful. Furthermore, in many cases investors have incentives to coordinate their choices. For example, someone who thinks other investors want to buy lots of Japanese yen may expect the yen to rise in value, and therefore has an incentive to buy yen too. Likewise, a depositor in Indy Mac Bank who expects other depositors to withdraw their funds may expect the bank to fail, and therefore has an incentive to withdraw too. Economists call an incentive to mimic the strategies of others as *strategic complementarities*.

It has been argued that if people or firms have a sufficiently strong incentive to do the same thing they expect others to do, then *self-fulfilling prophecies* may occur. For example, if investors expect the value of the yen to rise, this may cause its value to rise; and similarly, if depositors expect a bank to fail this may cause it to fail. Therefore, financial crises are sometimes viewed as a vicious circle in which investors shun some institution or asset because they expect others to do so.

Leverage

Leverage in the context of investment can be referred to as borrowing to finance investments. It is frequently cited as one of the contributor to financial crises. When a financial institution (or an individual) only invests its own money, it can, in the very worst case, lose its own money. But when it borrows in order to invest more, it can potentially earn more from its investment, but it can also lose more than all it has. Therefore, leverage magnifies the potential returns from investment, but also creates a risk of bankruptcy. Since bankruptcy means that a firm fails to honour all its promised payments to other firms, it may spread financial troubles from one firm to another.

The average degree of leverage in the economy often rises prior to a financial crisis. For example, borrowing to finance investment in the stock market ("margin buying") became increasingly common prior to the Wall Street Crash of 1929. Even in the recent market crash of 2008 it is said that significant number of investors have taken loan to finance their equity investment at the same time significant amount of transaction was going as margin trading in the stock market.

Asset-liability Mismatch

Another factor which is believed to contribute to financial crises is *asset-liability mismatch*. It is a situation in which the risks associated with an institution's debts and assets are not appropriately aligned. For example, commercial banks offer deposit accounts which can be withdrawn at any time and they use the proceeds to make long-term loans to businesses and homeowners. The mismatch between the banks' short-term liabilities (its deposits) and its long-term assets (its loans) is seen as one of the reason bank runs occur (when depositors panic and decide to withdraw their funds more quickly than the bank can get back the proceeds of its loans). Likewise, Bear Stearns failed in 2007-08 because it was unable to renew the short-term debt it used to finance long-term investments in mortgage securities.

In an international context, many emerging market governments are unable to sell bonds denominated in their own currencies, and therefore sell bonds denominated in US dollars instead. This generates a mismatch between the currency denomination of their liabilities (their bonds) and their assets (their local tax revenues), so that they run a risk of sovereign default due to fluctuations in exchange rates.

Uncertainty and Herd Behaviour

Many analyses of financial crises emphasize the role of investment mistakes caused by lack of knowledge or the imperfections of human reasoning. Behavioural finance studies show that herd behaviour is in the core of most of the financial crises. Psychologist Torbjorn K.A. Eliazonhas also analyzed failures of economic reasoning in his concept of 'œcopathy'.

Historians, notably Charles Kindleberger, have pointed out that crises often follow soon after major financial or technical innovations that present investors with new types of financial opportunities, which he called "displacements" of investors' expectations. Early examples include the South Sea Bubble and Mississippi Bubble of 1720, which occurred when the notion of investment in shares of company stock was itself new and unfamiliar, and the Crash of 1929, which followed the introduction of new electrical and transportation technologies. More recently, many financial crises followed changes in the investment environment brought about by financial deregulation, and the crash of the dot com bubble in 2001 arguably began with "irrational exuberance" about Internet technology.

Unfamiliarity with recent technical and financial innovations may help explain how investors sometimes grossly overestimate asset values. Also, if the first investors in a new class of assets (for example, stock in "dot com" companies) profit from rising asset values as other investors learn about the innovation (in our example, as others learn about the potential of the Internet), then still more others may follow their example, driving the price even higher as they rush to buy in hopes of similar profits. If such "herd behaviour" causes prices to spiral up far above the true value of the assets, a crash may become inevitable. If for any reason the price briefly falls, so that investors realize that further gains are not assured, then the spiral may go into reverse, with price decreases causing a rush of sales, reinforcing the decrease in prices.

Regulatory Failures

Many governments of the world have attempted to eliminate or mitigate financial crises by regulating the financial sector. One major goal of regulation is transparency. It means making institutions' financial situations publicly known by requiring regular reporting under standardized accounting procedures. Another goal of putting regulation is making sure institutions have sufficient assets to meet their contractual obligations, through reserve requirements, capital requirements, and other limits on leverage.

Some financial crises have been blamed on insufficient regulation, and have led to changes in regulation in order to avoid a repeat. For example, the Managing Director of the IMF, Dominique Strauss-Kahn, has blamed the financial crisis of 2008 on 'regulatory failure to guard against excessive risk-taking in the financial system, especially in the USA'. Likewise, the *New York Times* singled out the deregulation of credit default swaps as a cause of the crisis.

However, excessive regulation has also been cited as a possible cause of financial crises. In particular, the Basel II Accord has been criticized for requiring banks to increase their capital when risks rise. As a result, it might cause them to decrease lending precisely when capital is scarce and potentially aggravating a financial crisis.

Frauds

Fraud has played a role in the collapse of some financial institutions, when companies have attracted depositors with misleading claims about their investment strategies, or have embezzled the resulting income. Examples include Charles Ponzi's scam in early 20th century Boston, the collapse of the MMM investment fund in Russia in 1994, the scams that led to the Albanian Lottery Uprising of 1997, and, allegedly, the collapse of Madoff Investment Securities in 2008.

Many rogue traders that have caused large losses at financial institutions have been accused of acting fraudulently in order to hide their trades. Fraud in mortgage financing has also been cited as one possible cause of the 2008 sub-prime mortgage crisis. Government officials stated on Sept. 23, 2008 that the FBI was looking into possible fraud by mortgage financing companies Fannie Mae and Freddie Mac, Lehman Brothers, and insurer American International Group.

Contagion

Contagion refers to the idea that financial crises may spread from one institution to another, as when a bank run spreads from a few banks to many others, or from one country to another, as when currency crises, sovereign defaults, or stock market crashes spread across countries. When the failure of one particular financial institution threatens the stability of many other institutions, this is called *systemic risk* in this context.

One widely-cited example of contagion was the spread of the Thai crisis in 1997 to other countries of East Asia. However, economists often debate whether observing crises in many countries around the same time is truly caused by contagion from one market to another, or whether it is instead caused by similar underlying problems that would have affected each country individually even in the absence of international linkages.

Recessionary Effects

Some financial crises have little effect outside of the financial sector, like the Wall Street crash of 1987, but other crises are believed to have played a role in decreasing growth in the rest of the economy. There are many theories why a financial crisis could have a recessionary effect on the rest of the economy. These theoretical ideas include the 'financial accelerator', 'flight to quality' and 'flight to liquidity', and the Kiyotaki-Moore model. Some 'third generation' models of currency crises explore how currency crises and banking crises together can cause recessions.

THEORIES OF FINANCIAL CRISIS

World Systems Theory

Recurrent major depressions in the world economy after every 20 and 50 years have been the subject of empirical and econometric research especially in the world systems theory and in the debate about Nikolai Kondratiev and the so-called 50-years Kondratiev waves. Major figures of world systems theory, like Andre Gunder Frank and Immanuel Wallerstein, consistently warned about the crash that the world economy is now facing. World systems scholars and Kondratiev cycle researchers always implied that Washington Consensus-oriented economists never understood the dangers and perils, which leading industrial nations will be facing and are now facing at the end of the long economic cycle which began after the oil crisis of 1973.

Minsky's Theory

Hyman Minsky has proposed a post-Keynesian explanation that is most applicable to a closed economy. He theorized that financial fragility is a typical feature of any capitalist economy. High fragility leads to a higher risk of a financial crisis. To facilitate his analysis, Minsky defines three types of financing firms choose according to their tolerance of risk. They are hedge finance, speculative finance, and Ponzi finance. Ponzi finance leads to the most fragility.

Financial fragility levels move together with the business cycle. After a recession, firms have lost much financing and choose only hedge, the safest. As the economy grows and expected profits rise, firms tend to believe that they can allow themselves to take on speculative financing. In this case, they know that profits will not cover all the interest all the time. Firms, however, believe that profits will rise and the loans will eventually be repaid without much trouble. More loans lead to more investment, and the economy grows further. Then lenders also start believing that they will get back all the money they lend. Therefore, they are ready to lend to firms without full guarantees of success. Lenders know that such firms will have problems repaying. Still, they believe these firms will refinance from elsewhere as their expected profits rise. This is Ponzi financing. In this way, the economy has taken on much risky credit. Now it is only a question of time before some big firm actually defaults. Lenders understand the actual risks in the economy and stop giving credit so easily. Refinancing becomes impossible for many, and more firms default. If no new money comes into the economy to allow the refinancing process, a real economic crisis begins. During the recession, firms start to hedge again, and the cycle is closed.

Coordination Games

Mathematical approaches to modeling financial crises have emphasized that there is often positive feedback between market participants' decisions. Positive feedback implies that there may be dramatic changes in asset values in response to small changes in economic fundamentals. For example, some models of currency crises (including that of Paul Krugman) imply that a fixed exchange rate may be stable for a long period of time, but will collapse suddenly in an avalanche of currency sales in response to a sufficient deterioration of government finances or underlying economic conditions.

According to some theories, positive feedback implies that the economy can have more than one equilibrium. There may be an equilibrium in which market participants invest heavily in asset markets because they expect assets to be valuable, but there may be another equilibrium where participants flee asset markets because they expect others to flee too. This is the type of argument underlying Diamond and Dybvig's model of bank runs, in which savers withdraw their assets from the bank because they expect others to withdraw too. Likewise, in Obstfeld's model of currency crises, when economic conditions are neither too bad nor too good, there are two possible outcomes. Speculators may or may not decide to attack the currency depending on what they expect other speculators to do.

Herding Models and Learning Models

A variety of models have been developed in which asset values may spiral excessively up or down as investors learn from each other. In these models, asset purchases by a few agents encourage others to buy too, not because the true value of the asset increases when many buy (which is called "strategic complementarity"), but because investors come to believe the true asset value is high when they observe others buying.

In "herding" models, it is assumed that investors are fully rational, but only have partial information about the economy. In these models, when a few investors buy some type of asset, this reveals that they have some positive information about that asset, which increases the rational incentive of others to buy the asset too. Even though this is a fully rational decision, it may sometimes lead to mistakenly high asset values (implying, eventually, a crash) since the first investors may, by chance, have been mistaken.

In "adaptive learning" or "adaptive expectations" models, investors are assumed to be imperfectly rational, basing their reasoning only on recent experience. In such models, if the price of a given asset rises for some period of time, investors may begin to believe that its price always rises, which increases their tendency to buy and thus drives the price up further. Likewise, observing a few price decreases may give rise to a downward price spiral, so in models of this type large fluctuations in asset prices may occur. Agent-based models of financial markets often assume investors act on the basis of adaptive learning or adaptive expectations.

LIST OF FINANCIAL CRISES IN HISTORY

A short list of some major financial crises since 20th century:

- 1929: The Great Depression.
- 1980s: Latin American debt crisis, beginning in Mexico.
- 1989-91: United States Savings and Loan crisis.
- 1990s: Collapse of the Japanese asset price bubble.
- 1992-93: Speculative attacks on currencies in the European Exchange Rate Mechanism.
- 1994-95: Economic crisis in Mexico, speculative attack and default on Mexican debt.

- 1997-98: Asian Financial Crisis: devaluations and banking crises across Asia.
- 1998: Russian financial crisis: devaluation of the ruble and default on Russian debt.
- 2001-02: Argentine economic crisis (1999-2002): breakdown of banking system.
- 2008: Global financial crisis and USA, Europe: spread of the U.S. sub-prime mortgage crisis.

CONCLUSION

From the above discussions it is clear that the term financial crisis is not very uncommon in the history. There are many financial crises the world has faced till date. The causes of financial crisis every time may not be same, but the impact of the crisis is severe all the time. So, it better to understand the nature and causes of the crisis and take lessons from them so that the same kind of mistake is not repeated in the future.

The Great Depression

The *Great Depression* was the largest and most important economic depression in modern history. It was a phenomenon of worldwide economic downturn. It was started in most places in 1929 and ended at different times in the 1930s or early 1940s for different countries. The great depression of 1929 is used in the 21st century as an example of how far the world's economy can fall. It was originated in the United States. Historians most often use as a starting date of October 29, 1929, the day on which stock market crash and it is known as Black Tuesday.

Overview of the Chapter

The present chapter highlights about the great depression of 1929 which started in USA and gradually the whole world was being affected. The chapter highlights the following important headings:

- The Deflation Spiral
- Causes of the Great Depression
- The End of Great Depression
- Effects of the Great Depression
- The Scenario of 1937
- The Political Consequences
- Facts and Figures related to the Great Depression
- Other Great Depression
- Conclusion

The end of the depression in the U.S. is associated with the onset of the war economy of World War II, beginning around 1939.

The depression had devastating effects in virtually every country, rich or poor. International trade plunged by half to two-thirds. The similar kind of effect was there on personal income, tax revenue, prices and profits. Cities all around the world were hit hard, especially those dependent on heavy industry. Construction was virtually halted in many countries. Farming and rural areas suffered as crop prices fell by roughly 60 percent. Facing plummeting demand with few alternate sources of jobs, areas dependent on primary sector industries such as farming, mining and logging suffered the most. The Great Depression ended at different times in different countries. The majority of countries set-up relief programs, and most underwent some sort of political upheaval, pushing them to the left or right.

THE DEFLATION SPIRAL

The Great Depression was triggered by a sudden, total collapse in the stock market on October 29, 1929. The stock market turned upward in early 1930, returning to early 1929 levels by April, though still almost 30 percent below the peak of September 1929. Together, government and business actually spent more in the first half of 1930 than in the corresponding period of the previous year. But consumers, many of whom had suffered severe losses in the stock market in the previous year, cut back their expenditures significantly, and a severe drought ravaged the agricultural heartland of the USA beginning in the summer of 1930.

In early 1930, credit was ample and available at low rates, but people were reluctant to add new debt by borrowing. By May 1930, auto sales had declined to below the levels of 1928. Prices in general began to decline, but wages held steady in 1930, then began to drop in 1931. Conditions were worse in farming areas, where commodity prices plunged, and in mining and logging areas, where unemployment was high and there were few other jobs. The decline in the US economy was the factor that pulled down most other countries at first, and then internal weaknesses or strengths in each country made conditions worse or better. By late in 1930, a steady decline have reached bottom by March 1933.

CAUSES OF THE GREAT DEPRESSION

There were multiple causes for the first downturn in 1929. These include the structural weaknesses and specific events that turned it into a major depression and the way in which the downturn spread from country to country. In relation to the 1929 downturn, historians emphasize structural factors like massive bank failures and the stock market crash, while economists point to Britain's decision to return to the Gold Standard at pre-World War I parities (US$ 4.86:£1).

Free Market or Government Failure : The Debate Continues

Recession cycles are thought to be a normal part of living in a world of inexact balances between supply and demand. But what turns a usually mild and short recession or "ordinary" business cycle into a great depression is a subject of debate and concern. Scholars have not agreed on the exact causes and their relative importance. The search for causes is closely connected to the question of how to avoid a future depression, and so the political and policy viewpoints of scholars are mixed into the analysis of historic events eight decades ago. The even larger question is whether it was largely a failure on the part of free markets or largely a failure on the part of governments to curtail widespread bank failures, the resulting panics, and reduction in the money supply. Those who believe in a large role for the state in the economy believe it was mostly a failure of the free markets and those who believe in free markets believe it was mostly a failure of government that compounded the problem.

What Theories Say

Current theories related to the great depression may be broadly classified into three main categories. First, there is orthodox classical economics, i.e., monetarist, Austrian Economics and neoclassical economic theory, all of which focus on the macroeconomic effects of money supply and the supply of gold which backed many currencies before the Great Depression, including production and consumption.

Second, there are structural theories, most importantly Keynesian, but also including those of institutional economics, that point to under consumption and overinvestment (economic bubble), malfeasance by bankers and industrialists, or incompetence by government officials. The only consensus viewpoint is that there was a large-scale lack of confidence. Unfortunately, once panic and deflation set in, many people believed they could make more money by keeping clear of the markets as prices got lower and lower and a given amount of money bought ever more goods.

Third, there is the Marxist critique of political economy. This emphasizes the tendency of capitalism to create unbalanced accumulations of wealth, leading to over accumulations of capital and a repeating cycle of devaluations through economic crises. Marx saw recession and depression as unavoidable under free-market capitalism as there are no restrictions on accumulations of capital other than the market itself.

Debt Deflation

Irving Fisher argued that the predominant factor leading to the Great Depression was over indebtedness and deflation. Fisher tied loose credit to over-indebtedness, which fueled speculation and asset bubbles. He then outlined 9 factors interacting with one another under conditions of debt and deflation to create the mechanics of boom to bust. The chain of events proceeded as follows:

1. Debt liquidation and distress selling.
2. Contraction of the money supply as bank loans are paid-off.
3. A fall in the level of asset prices.
4. A still greater fall in the net worth of business, precipitating bankruptcies.
5. A fall in profits.
6. A reduction in output, in trade and in employment.
7. Pessimism and loss of confidence.

8. Hoarding of money.
9. A fall in nominal interest rates and a rise in deflation adjusted interest rates.

During the Crash of 1929 preceding the Great Depression, margin requirements were only 10%. Brokerage firms, in other words, would lend $ 9 for every $ 1 an investor had deposited. When the market fell, brokers called in these loans, which could not be paid back. Banks began to fail as debtors defaulted on debt and depositors attempted to withdraw their deposits in masses, triggering multiple bank runs. Government guarantees and Federal Reserve banking regulations to prevent such panics were ineffective or not used. Bank failures led to the loss of billions of dollars in assets. Outstanding debts became heavier, because prices and incomes fell by 20–50% but the debts remained at the same dollar amount. After the panic of 1929, and during the first 10 months of 1930, 744 US banks failed. (In all, 9,000 banks failed during the 1930s). By April 1933, around $ 7 billion in deposits had been frozen in failed banks or those left unlicensed after the March Bank Holiday.

Bank failures snow balled as desperate bankers called in loans which the borrowers did not have time or money to repay. With future profits looking poor, capital investment and construction slowed or completely ceased. In the face of bad loans and worsening future prospects, the surviving banks became even more conservative in their lending. Banks built up their capital reserves and made fewer loans, which intensified deflationary pressures. A vicious cycle developed and the downward spiral accelerated.

The liquidation of debt could not keep up with the fall of prices which it caused. The mass effect of the stampede to liquidate increased the value of each dollar owed, relative to the value of declining asset holdings. The very effort of individuals to lessen their burden of debt effectively increased it. Paradoxically, the more the debtors paid, the more they owed. This self-aggravating process turned a 1930 recession into a 1933 great depression. Macroeconomists including Ben Bernanke, then chairman of the U.S. Federal Reserve Bank, have revived the debt-deflation view of the Great Depression originated by Fisher.

Trade Decline and the U.S. Smoot-Hawley Tariff Act

Many economists have argued that the sharp decline in international trade after 1930 helped to worsen the depression. The impact was especially more for countries significantly dependent on foreign trade. Most historians and economists partly blame the American Smoot-Hawley Tariff Act (enacted June 17, 1930) for worsening the depression by seriously reducing international trade and causing retaliatory tariffs in other countries. Foreign trade was a small part of overall economic activity in the United States and was concentrated in a few businesses like farming. But it was a much larger factor in many other countries. The average *ad valorem* rate of duties on dutiable imports for 1921-25 was 25.9% but under the new tariff it jumped to 50% in 1931-35.

In dollar terms, American exports declined from about $ 5.2 billion in 1929 to $ 1.7 billion in 1933; but prices also fell at the same time, so the physical volume of exports only fell by half. Hardest hit were farm commodities such as wheat, cotton, tobacco, and lumber. According to this theory, the collapse of farm exports caused many American farmers to default on their loans, leading to the bank runs on small rural banks that characterized the early years of the Great Depression.

U.S. Federal Reserve and Money Supply

Monetarists, including Milton Friedman and current Federal Reserve System chairman Ben Bernanke, argue that the Great Depression was caused by monetary contraction, the consequence of poor policy-making by the American Federal Reserve System and continuous crisis in the banking system. In this view, the Federal Reserve, by not acting, allowed the money supply as measured by the M2 to shrink by one-third from 1929 to 1933. Friedman argued that the downward turn in the economy, starting with the stock market crash, would have been just another recession. The problem was that some large, public bank failures, particularly that of the New York Bank of the United States, produced panic and widespread runs on local banks, and that the Federal Reserve sat idly by while banks fell. He claimed that, if the Fed had provided emergency lending to these key banks, or simply bought government bonds on the open market to provide liquidity and increase the quantity of money after the key banks fell, all the rest of the banks would not have fallen after the large ones did, and the money supply would not have fallen as far and as fast as it did. With significantly less money to go around, businessmen could not get new loans and could not even get their old loans renewed, forcing many to stop investing. This interpretation blames the Federal Reserve for inaction, especially the New York branch.

One reason why the Federal Reserve did not act to limit the decline of the money supply was regulation. At that time the amount of credit the Federal Reserve could issue was limited by laws which required partial gold backing of that credit. By the late 1920s the Federal Reserve had almost hit the limit of allowable credit that could be backed by the gold in its possession. This credit was in the form of Federal Reserve demand notes. Since a "promise of gold" is not as good as "gold in the hand", during the bank panics a portion of those demand notes were redeemed for Federal Reserve gold. Since the Federal Reserve had hit its limit on allowable credit, any reduction in gold in its vaults had to be accompanied by a greater reduction in credit. On April 5, 1933 President Roosevelt signed Executive Order 6102 making the private ownership of gold illegal, reducing the pressure on Federal Reserve Gold.

Austrian School Explanations

Another explanation comes from the Austrian School of economics. Theorists of the "Austrian School" who wrote about the Depression include Austrian economist Friedrich Hayek and American economist Murray Rothbard, who wrote *America's Great Depression* (1963). In their view, the key cause of the Depression was the expansion of the money supply in the 1920s that led to an unsustainable credit-driven boom. In their view, the Federal Reserve, which was created in 1913, shoulders much of the blame.

One reason for the monetary inflation was to help Great Britain, which, in the 1920s, was struggling with its plans to return to the gold standard at pre-war (World War I) parity. Returning to the gold standard at this rate meant that the

British economy was facing deflationary pressure. According to Rothbard, the lack of price flexibility in Britain meant that unemployment shot up, and the American government was asked to help. The United States was receiving a net inflow of gold, and inflated further in order to help Britain return to the gold standard. Montagu Norman, head of the Bank of England, had an especially good relationship with Benjamin Strong, the *de facto* head of the Federal Reserve. Norman pressured the heads of the central banks of France and Germany to inflate as well, but unlike Strong, they refused. Rothbard says American inflation was meant to allow Britain to inflate as well, because under the gold standard, Britain could not inflate on its own.

According to the Austrian view, it was this inflation of the money supply that led to an unsustainable boom in both asset prices (stocks and bonds) and capital goods. By the time the Fed belatedly tightened in 1928, it was far too late and, in the Austrian view, a depression was inevitable.

The artificial interference in the economy was a disaster prior to the Depression, and government efforts to prop up the economy after the crash of 1929 only made things worse. According to Rothbard, government intervention delayed the market's adjustment and made the road to complete recovery more difficult.

Furthermore, Rothbard criticizes Milton Friedman's assertion that the central bank failed to inflate the supply of money. Rothbard asserts that the Federal Reserve bought $ 1.1 billion of government securities from February to July 1932, raising its total holding to $ 1.8 billion. Total bank reserves rose by only $ 212 million, but Rothbard argues that this was because the American populace lost faith in the banking system and began hoarding more cash, a factor quite beyond the control of the Central Bank. The potential for a run on the banks caused local bankers to be more conservative in lending out their reserves, and this, Rothbard argues, was the cause of the Federal Reserve's inability to inflate.

Role of Business Houses

Franklin D. Roosevelt became the US president in 1932. He primarily blamed the excesses of big business for causing an unstable bubble-like economy. Democrats believed the problem was that business had too much money, and the New Deal was intended as a remedy, by empowering labor unions and farmers and by raising taxes on corporate profits. Regulation of the economy was a favorite remedy. Some New Deal regulation was declared unconstitutional by the U.S. Supreme Court. Most New Deal regulations were abolished or scaled back in the 1970s and 1980s in a bipartisan wave of deregulation. However, the Securities and Exchange Commission and Social Security won widespread support.

Lack of Government Deficit Spending

British economist John Maynard Keynes argued in General Theory of Employment Interest and Money that lower aggregate expenditures in the economy contributed to a massive decline in income and to employment that was well below the average. In this situation, the economy might have reached a perfect balance, at a cost of high unemployment. Keynesian economists called on governments during times of economic crisis to pick-up the slack by increasing government spending and/or cutting taxes.

Massive increases in deficit spending, new banking regulation, and boosting farm prices did start turning the U.S. economy around in 1933, but it was a slow and painful process. The U.S. had not returned to 1929's GNP for over a decade and still had an unemployment rate of about 15% in 1940—down from 25% in 1933.

Inequality of Wealth and Income

Marriner S. Eccles, who served as Franklin D. Roosevelt's Chairman of the Federal Reserve from November 1934 to February 1948, detailed what he believed caused the Depression in his memoirs, Beckoning Frontiers (New York, Alfred A. Knopf, 1951). *"As mass production has to be accompanied by mass consumption, mass consumption, in turn, implies a distribution of wealth—not of existing wealth, but of wealth as it is currently produced—to provide men with buying power equal to the amount of goods and services offered by the nation's economic machinery."*

Instead of achieving that kind of distribution, a giant suction pump had by 1929-30 drawn into a few hands an increasing portion of currently produced wealth. This served them as capital accumulations. But by taking purchasing power out of the hands of mass consumers, the savers denied to themselves the kind of effective demand for their products that would justify a reinvestment of their capital accumulations in new plants. In consequence, as in a poker game where the chips were concentrated in fewer and fewer hands, the other fellows could stay in the game only by borrowing. When their credit ran out, the game stopped. That is what happened to USA in the twenties. They sustained high levels of employment in that period with the aid of an exceptional expansion of debt outside of the banking system. This debt was provided by the large growth of business savings as well as savings by individuals, particularly in the upper-income groups where taxes were relatively low. Private debt outside of the banking system increased about fifty per cent. This debt, which was at high interest rates, largely took the form of mortgage debt on housing, office, and hotel structures, consumer instalment debt, brokers' loans, and foreign debt. The stimulation to spend by debt-creation of this sort was short-lived and could not be counted on to sustain high levels of employment for long periods of time. Had there been a better distribution of the current income from the national product—in other words, had there been less savings by business and the higher-income groups and more income in the lower groups—there could have had far greater stability in their economy. Had the six billion dollars, for instance, that were loaned by corporations and wealthy individuals for stock-market speculation been distributed to the public as lower prices or higher wages and with less profits to the corporations and the well-to-do, it would have prevented or greatly moderated the economic collapse that began at the end of 1929.

The time came when there were no more poker chips to be loaned on credit. Debtors thereupon were forced to curtail their consumption in an effort to create a margin that could be applied to the reduction of outstanding debts. This naturally reduced the demand for goods of all kinds and brought on what seemed to be overproduction, but was in reality under consumption when judged in terms of the real world instead of the money world. This, in turn, brought about a fall in prices and employment.

Unemployment further decreased the consumption of goods, which further increased unemployment, thus closing the circle in a continuing decline of prices. Earnings began to disappear, requiring economies of all kinds in the wages, salaries, and time of those employed. And thus again the vicious circle of deflation was closed until one third of the entire working population was unemployed, with the national income reduced by fifty per cent, and with the aggregate debt burden greater than ever before, not in dollars, but measured by current values and income that represented the ability to pay. Fixed charges, such as taxes, railroad and other utility rates, insurance and interest charges, clung close to the 1929 level and required such a portion of the national income to meet them that the amount left for consumption of goods was not sufficient to support the population.

THE END OF GREAT DEPRESSION

The turning point in the depression was in 1933. Some economists attribute the subsequent recovery to monetary expansion that began after the bank holiday a few days after Roosevelt has taken charge on March 4, 1933 and devaluation of the U.S. dollar that was then tied to gold.

The massive rearmament policies to counter the threat from Nazi Germany helped stimulate the economies of Europe in 1937-39. By 1937, unemployment in Britain had fallen to 1.5 million. The mobilization of manpower following the outbreak of war in 1939 finally ended unemployment.

In the United States, the massive war spending doubled the GNP, either masking the effects of the Depression or essentially ending the Depression. Businessmen ignored the mounting national debt and heavy new taxes, redoubling their efforts for greater output to take advantage of generous government contracts. As a result, productivity soared and most people worked overtime and gave up leisure activities to make money after so many hard years. People accepted rationing and price controls for the first time as a way of expressing their support for the war effort. Cost-plus pricing in munitions contracts guaranteed businesses a profit no matter how many mediocre workers they employed or how inefficient the techniques they used. The demand was for a vast quantity of war supplies as soon as possible, regardless of cost. Businesses hired every person in sight, even driving sound trucks up and down city streets begging people to apply for jobs. New workers were needed to replace the 11 million working-age men serving in the military. These events magnified the role of the federal government in the national economy. In 1929, federal expenditures accounted for only 3% of GNP. Between 1933 and 1939, federal expenditure tripled, and Roosevelt's critics charged that he was turning America into a socialist state.

EFFECTS OF THE GREAT DEPRESSION

Australia

Australia's extreme dependence on agricultural and industrial exports meant it was one of the hardest-hit countries in the Western world, amongst the likes of Canada and Germany. Falling export demand and commodity prices placed massive downward pressures on wages. Further, unemployment reached a record high of 29% in 1932, with incidents of civil unrest becoming common. After 1932, an increase in wool and meat prices led to a gradual recovery.

Canada

Harshly impacted by both the global economic downturn and the Dust Bowl, Canadian industrial production had fallen to only 58% of the 1929 level by 1932, the second lowest level in the world after the United States, and well behind nations such as Britain, which saw it fall only to 83% of the 1929 level. Total national income fell to 56% of the 1929 level, again worse than any nation apart from the United States. Unemployment reached 27% at the depth of the Depression in 1933. During the 1930s, Canada employed a highly restrictive immigration policy.

France

The Depression began to affect France around 1931. France's relatively high degree of self-sufficiency meant the damage was considerably less than in nations like Germany. However, hardship and unemployment were high enough to lead to rioting and the rise of the socialist Popular Front.

Germany

Germany's Weimar Republic was hit hard by the depression, as American loans to help rebuild the German economy now stopped. Unemployment soared, especially in larger cities, and the political system veered toward extremism. The unemployment rate reached nearly 30% in 1932. Repayment of the war reparations due by Germany were suspended in 1932 following the Lausanne Conference of 1932. By that time Germany had repaid 1/8th of the reparations. Hitler's Nazi Party came to power in January 1933.

Japan

The Great Depression did not strongly affect Japan. The Japanese economy shrank by 8% during 1929–31. However, Japan's Minister of Finance (MoF) Osachi Hamaguchi implemented the first version of Keynesian economic policies. First, by increasing deficit spending; and second, by devaluing the currency. The MoF believed that the deficit spending could easily be paid for when productivity improved.

The devaluation of the currency had an immediate effect. Japanese textiles began to displace British textiles in export markets. The deficit spending however proved to be most profound. The deficit spending went into the purchase of munitions for the armed forces. By 1933, Japan was already out of the depression. By 1934 the MoF realized that the economy was in danger of overheating, and to avoid inflation, moved to reduce the deficit spending that went towards armaments and ammunitions. This resulted in a strong and swift negative reaction from nationalists, especially those in the Army, culminating in an assassination attempt on the MoF, leading to his eventual demise from poor health some months later. This had a chilling effect on all civilian bureaucrats in the

Japanese government. From 1934, the military's dominance of the government continued to grow. Instead of reducing deficit spending, the government introduced price controls and rationing schemes that reduced, but did not eliminate inflation, which would remain a problem until the end of World War II.

The deficit spending had a transformative effect on Japan. Japan's industrial production doubled during the 1930s. Further, in 1929 the list of the largest firms in Japan was dominated by light industries, especially textile companies (many of Japan's automakers, like Toyota, have their roots in the textile industry). By 1940 light industry had been displaced by heavy industry as the largest firms inside the Japanese economy.

Latin America

Because of high levels of United States investment in Latin American economies, they were severely damaged by the Depression. Within the region, Chile, Bolivia and Peru were particularly badly affected.

Netherlands

From roughly 1931 until 1937, the Netherlands suffered a deep and exceptionally long depression. This depression was partly caused by the after-effects of the Stock Market Crash of 1929 in the United States, and partly by internal factors in the Netherlands. Government policy, especially the very late dropping of the Gold Standard, played a role in prolonging the depression. The Great Depression in the Netherlands led to some political instability and riots, and can be linked to the rise of the Dutch national-socialist party [NSB]. The depression in the Netherlands eased-off somewhat at the end of 1936, when the government finally dropped the Gold Standard, but real economic stability did not return until after World War II.

South Africa

As world trade slumped, demand for South African agricultural and mineral exports fell drastically. The Carnegie Commission on Poor Whites had concluded in 1931 that nearly one-third of Afrikaners lived as paupers. It is believed that the social discomfort caused by the depression was a contributing factor in the 1933 split between the "gesuiwerde" (purified) and "smelter" (fusionist) factions within the National Party and the National Party's subsequent fusion with the South African Party.

Soviet Union

Having removed itself from the capitalist world system both by choice and as a result of efforts of the capitalist powers to isolate it, the Great Depression had little effect on the Soviet Union. A Soviet trade agency in New York advertised 6,000 positions and received more than 100,000 applications. This was a period of industrial expansion for the USSR as it recovered from revolution and civil war, and its apparent immunity to the Great Depression seemed to validate the theory of Marxism and contributed to Socialist and Communist agitation in affected nations. This in turn increased fears of Communist revolution in the West, strengthening support for anti-Communists, both moderate and extreme. Unlike the previous similar famine in Russia, information about the Soviet famine of 1932-33 was suppressed by the Soviet authorities until perestroika. In 1933 workers' real earnings sank to about one-tenth of the 1926 level. Common and political prisoners in labour camps were forced to do unpaid labour, and communists and Komsomol members were frequently "mobilized" for various construction projects.

United Kingdom

The effects on the industrial areas of Britain were immediate and devastating, as demand for British products collapsed. By the end of 1930 unemployment had more than doubled from 1 million to 2.5 million (20% of the insured workforce), and exports had fallen in value by 50%. In 1933, 30% of Glaswegians were unemployed due to the severe decline in heavy industry. In some towns and cities in the north east, unemployment reached as high as 70% as ship production fell 90%. About 200,000 unemployed men were sent to the work camps, which continued in operation until 1939.

United States

Early Response

Secretary of the Treasury Andrew Mellon advised President Hoover that shock treatment would be the best response. "Liquidate labour, liquidate stocks, liquidate the farmers, and liquidate real estate. That will purge the rottenness out of the system. High costs of living and high living will come down. People will work harder, live a more moral life. Values will be adjusted, and enterprising people will pick up the wrecks from less competent people." Hoover rejected this advice, and started numerous programs, all of which failed to reverse the downturn.

Hoover launched a series of programs to increase farm prices, which failed, expanded federal spending in public works such as dams, and launched the Reconstruction Finance Corporation (RFC) which aided cities, banks and railroads, and continued as a major agency under the New Deal. To provide unemployment relief he set-up the Emergency Relief Agency (ERA) that operated until 1935 as the Federal Emergency Relief Agency. Quarter by quarter the economy went downhill, as prices, profits and employment fell, leading to the political realignment in 1932 that brought to power the New Deal.

The New Deal

Shortly after President Roosevelt has taken charge in 1933, drought and erosion combined to cause the Dust Bowl, shifting hundreds of thousands of displaced persons off their farms in the mid west. From his inauguration onward, Roosevelt argued that restructuring of the economy would be needed to prevent another depression or avoid prolonging the current one. New Deal programs sought to stimulate demand and provide work and relief for the impoverished through increased government spending and institute financial reforms. The Securities Act of 1933 comprehensively regulated the securities industry. This was followed by the Securities Exchange Act of 1934 which created the Securities and Exchange Commission. Even after the amendments, key provisions of both acts are still in force. Federal insurance of bank deposits was provided by the FDIC, and the Glass-

Steagall Act. The institution of the National Recovery Administration (NRA) remains a controversial act to this day. The NRA made a number of sweeping changes to the American economy until it was deemed unconstitutional by the Supreme Court of the United States in 1935.

Early changes by the Roosevelt administration included:

- Instituting regulations to fight deflationary "cut-throat competition" through the NRA.
- Setting minimum prices and wages, labour standards, and competitive conditions in all industries through the NRA.
- Encouraging unions that would raise wages, to increase the purchasing power of the working class.
- Cutting farm production to raise prices through the Agricultural Adjustment Act and its successors.
- Forcing businesses to work with government to set price codes through the NRA.

These reforms, together with several other relief and recovery measures are called the First New Deal. New regulations and attempts at economic stimulus through a new alphabet soup of agencies set-up in 1933 and 1934 and previously extant agencies such as the Reconstruction Finance Corporation brought a sharp upswing of the economy, with GDP returning to the levels of the late 1920s. By 1935, the "Second New Deal" added Social Security (which did not start making large payouts until much later), a jobs program for the unemployed (the Works Progress Administration, WPA) and, through the National Labour Relations Board, a strong stimulus to the growth of labour unions. Unemployment declined by over one-third in Roosevelt's first term (from 25% to 14.3%, 1933 to 1937). In Roosevelt's second term, the economy went into a short, sharp recession in 1937-38. In 1929, federal expenditures constituted only 3% of the GDP. The national debt as a proportion of GNP rose under Hoover from 20% to 40%. Roosevelt kept it at 40% until the war began, when it soared to 128%. After the Recession of 1937, conservatives were able to form a bipartisan conservative coalition to stop further expansion of the New Deal and, when unemployment dropped to 2% they abolished WPA, CCC and the PWA relief programs; Social Security, however, remained in place.

THE SCENARIO OF 1937

In 1937 the American economy took an unexpected nosedive, lasting through most of 1938. Production declined sharply, as did profits and employment. Unemployment jumped from 14.3% in 1937 to 19.0% in 1938. The Roosevelt administration reacted by launching a rhetorical campaign against monopoly power, which was cast as the cause of the depression, and by appointing Thurman Arnold to act; Arnold's effectiveness ended once World War II began and corporate energies had to be directed to winning the war.

The administration's other response to the 1937 deepening of the Great Depression had more tangible results. Ignoring the pleas of the Treasury Department, Roosevelt embarked on an antidote to the depression, reluctantly abandoning his efforts to balance the budget and launching a $ 5 billion spending program in the spring of 1938, an effort to increase mass purchasing power. Business-oriented observers explained the recession and recovery in very different terms from the Keynesians. They argued that the New Deal had been very hostile to business expansion in 1935–37, had encouraged massive strikes which had a negative impact on major industries such as automobiles, and had threatened massive antitrust legal attacks on big corporations. All those threats diminished sharply after 1938. For example, the antitrust efforts fizzled out without major cases. The CIO and AFL unions started battling each other more than with the corporations, and tax policy became more favourable to long-term growth, according to this argument.

On the other hand, according to economist Robert Higgs, when looking only at the supply of consumer goods, significant GDP growth resumed only in 1946 (Higgs does not estimate the value to consumers of collective, intangible goods like victory in war). To some Keynesians, the war economy showed just how large the fiscal stimulus required to end the downturn of the Depression was, and it led, at the time, to fears that as soon as America demobilized, it would return to Depression conditions, and industrial output would fall to pre-war levels. That Keynesian prediction that a new depression would start after the war failed to take into account massive savings and pent-up consumer demand, along with the ending of the restrictive wartime regulations in most consumer industries, and the cutting of high tax rates starting in 1946. In any case, government spending and changing regulations (first tightening them, and then loosening them) appear to have contributed to the recovery, as consumer and producer behavior changed.

THE POLITICAL IMPLICATIONS

The crisis had many political consequences, among which was the abandonment of classic economic liberal approaches, which Roosevelt replaced in the United States with Keynesian policies. It was a main factor in the implementation of social democracy and planned economies in European countries after World War II. Although Austrian economists had challenged Keynesianism since the 1920s, it was not until the 1970s, with the influence of Milton Friedman that the Keynesian approach was politically questioned, leading the way to neo-liberalism.

THE FACTS AND FIGURES

Effects of depression in the United States:

- 13 million people became unemployed. In 1932, 34 million people belonged to families with no regular full-time wage earner.
- Industrial production fell by nearly 45% between the years 1929 and 1932.
- Homebuilding dropped by 80% between the years 1929 and 1932.
- In the 1920s, the banking system in the U.S. was about $ 50 billion, which was about 50% of GDP.
- From the years 1929 to 1932, about 5,000 banks went out of business.

- By 1933, 11,000 of the US 25,000 banks had failed.
- Between 1929 and 1933, U.S. GDP fell around 30%, the stock market lost almost 90% of its value.
- In 1929, the unemployment rate averaged 3%.
- In 1933, 25% of all workers and 37% of all non farm workers were unemployed.
- In Cleveland, Ohio, the unemployment rate was 60%; in Toledo, Ohio, 80%.
- One Soviet trading corporation in New York averaged 350 applications a day from Americans seeking jobs in the Soviet Union.
- Over one million families lost their farms between 1930 and 1934.
- Corporate profits had dropped from $ 10 billion three years ago to $ 1billion in 1932.
- Between 1929 and 1932 the income of the average American family was reduced by 40%.
- Nine million savings accounts had been wiped out between 1930 and 1933.
- 273,000 families had been evicted from their homes in 1932.
- There were two million homeless people migrating around the country.
- One Arkansas man walked 900 miles looking for work.
- Over 60% of Americans were categorized as poor by the federal government in 1933.
- In the last prosperous year (1929), there were 279,678 immigrants recorded, but in 1933 only 23,068 came to the U.S.
- In the early 1930s, more people emigrated from the United States than immigrated to it.
- New York social workers reported that 25% of all schoolchildren were malnourished. In the mining counties of West Virginia, Illinois, Kentucky, and Pennsylvania, the proportion of malnourished children was perhaps as high as 90%.
- Many people became ill with diseases such as tuberculosis (TB).

- The 1930 U.S. Census determined the U.S. population to be 122,775,046. About 40% of the population was under 20 years.

OTHER SIMILAR DEPRESSIONS

There have been other downturns called a "Great Depression," but none has been as worldwide for so long. British economic historians use the term "Great depression" to describe British conditions in the late 19th century, especially in agriculture, 1873-96, a period also referred to as the Long Depression. Several Latin American countries had severe downturns in the 1980s. Finnish economists refer to the Finnish economic decline around the breakup of the Soviet Union (1989-94) as a great depression. Kehoe and Prescott define a great depression to be a period of diminished economic output with at least one year where output is 20% below the trend. By this definition Argentina, Brazil, Chile, and Mexico experienced great depressions in the 1980s, and Argentina experienced another in 1998-2002. This definition also includes the economic performance of New Zealand from 1974-92 and Switzerland from 1973 to the present, although this designation for Switzerland has been controversial.

The economic crisis in the 1990s that struck former members of the Soviet Union was almost twice as intense as the Great Depression in the countries of Western Europe and the United States in the 1930s. Average standards of living registered a catastrophic fall in the early 1990s in many parts of the former Eastern Bloc-most notably, in post-Soviet states. Even before Russia's financial crisis of 1998, Russia's GDP was half of what it had been in the early 1990s. Some populations are still poorer today than they were in 1989 (e.g. Ukraine, Moldova, Serbia, Central Asia, and Caucasus). The collapse of the Soviet planned economy and the transition to market economy resulted in catastrophic declines in GDP of about 45% during the 1990-96 periods and poverty in the region had increased more than ten-fold.

CONCLUSION

It is observed in the above paragraphs that the great depression is one such depression in the history which has such a devastating effect both in terms of economics, politics as well as on the normal human activity. The depression was the result of some of the mistakes done by the policy-makers of those times. One should learn lesson from those mistakes and see to it that the same mistakes are not repeated again in the future. As it is said that prevention is better than cure, this proverb is also equally applicable in this case. This also gives us one lesson that depressions will come and go but prosperity has always returned.

3 Latin American Debt Crisis

Overview of the Chapter

This chapter of the book deals with the Latin American Debt Crisis of 1970-80s. The major highlights of the chapter are as follows:

- Origin of the Crisis
- Beginning of the Debt Crisis and Effects
- Current Level of External Debt of Latin American Countries
- Conclusion

The Latin America was also affected by the financial crisis during the 1970s and 80s. It was primarily a debt crisis and that is why it is called as Latin American Debt Crisis. The *Latin American debt crisis* was a financial crisis that occurred in the early 1980s (and for some countries starting in the 1970s). This period is also often referred to as the "lost decade". The crisis was primarily due to the fact that the Latin American countries have reached a point where their foreign debt over a period of time exceeded their earning power and as a result they were not able to repay it.

ORIGIN OF THE CRISIS

During the period of 1960s and 1970s many Latin American countries, notably Brazil, Argentina, and Mexico, borrowed huge sums of money from international creditors like IMF and World Bank for industrialization; especially for infrastructure programs. These countries had soaring economies at that time so the creditors were happy to continue to provide loans. Between 1975 and 1982, Latin American debt of commercial banks increased at a cumulative annual rate of 20.4 percent. This heightened borrowing led Latin America to quadruple its external debt from $ 75 billion in 1975 to more than $ 315 billion in 1983, or 50 percent of the region's gross domestic product (GDP). Debt service (interest payments and the repayment of principal) grew even faster, reaching $ 66 billion in 1982, up from $ 12 billion in 1975. All these have made the situation worse and laid the foundation of the debt crisis in Latin American countries.

BEGINNING OF THE DEBT CRISIS AND EFFECTS

During 1970s and 1980s, the world economy went into recession and at the same time the oil prices skyrocketed. It has created a breaking point for most countries in the region of Latin America. Developing countries also found themselves in a desperate liquidity crunch. Petroleum exporting countries flush with cash after the oil price increases of 1973-74. They invested their money with international banks, which 'recycled' a major portion of that money as loans to Latin American governments. As interest rates increased in the United States of America and in Europe in 1979, debt payments also increased making it harder for borrowing countries to pay back their debts. While the dangerous accumulation of foreign debt occurred over a number of years, the debt crisis began when the international capital markets became aware that Latin America would not be able to pay back its loans. This occurred in August 1982 when Mexico's Finance Minister, Jesus Silva-Herzog declared that Mexico would no longer be able to service its debt. In the wake of Mexico's default, most commercial banks reduced significantly or halted new lending to Latin America. As most of the loans of Latin America were short-term, a crisis ensued when their refinancing was refused by the financial institutions.

As a result, billions of dollars of loans that previously would have been refinanced were now due immediately.

In response to the crisis, most nations abandoned their import substitution industrialization models of economy and adopted an export-oriented industrialization strategy, usually the neo-liberal strategy encouraged by the IMF, though there are exceptions such as Chile and Costa Rica who adopted reformist strategies. A massive process of capital outflow, particularly to the United States, served to depreciate the exchange rates, thereby raising the real interest rate. Real GDP

TABLE 3.1
List of Countries with External Debt

Rank	*Country–Entity*	*External Debt (million US$)*	*Date of Iinformation*
22	Brazil	211,400	30 June 2005 est.
24	Mexico	174,300	30 June 2005 est.
29	Argentina	119,000	June 2005 est.
39	Chile	44,800	31 October 2005 est.
43	Venezuela	39,790	2005 est.
45	Colombia	37,060	30 June 2005 est.
50	Peru	30,180	30 June 2005 est.
65	Ecuador	17,010	31 December 2004 est.
73	Cuba	13,100	2005 est.
79	Uruguay	9,931	30 June 2005 est.
81	Panama	9,859	2005 est.
85	El Salvador	8,273	30 June 2005 est.
88	Dominican Republic	7,907	2005 est.
95	Bolivia	6,430	2005 est.
98	Guatemala	5,503	2005 est.
103	Honduras	4,675	2005 est.
108	Nicaragua	4,054	2005 est.
110	Costa Rica	3,633	30 June 2005 est.
112	Paraguay	3,535	2005 est.

growth rate for the region was only 2.3 percent between 1980 and 1985, but in per capita terms Latin America experienced negative growth of almost 9 percent.

The debt crisis is one of the elements which contributed to the collapse of some authoritarian dictatorships in the region, such as Brazil's military regime and the Argentine bureaucratic-authoritarian regime.

CURRENT LEVEL OF EXTERNAL DEBTS

Since the 1980 several countries in the region have experienced a surge in economic development and have initiated debt management programs in addition to debt relief and debt rescheduling programs agreed to by their international creditors. However, the debt crisis continues to have enduring effects, including the USD 2.94 trillion of Latin American and Caribbean debt traded globally in 2004, accounting for 63.2% of total emerging markets debt traded worldwide that year. The following is a list of external debt for Latin America based on a March 2006 report by The World Fact book.

CONCLUSION

The chapter discusses in brief about the debt crisis of the Latin American Countries in the 1970s and 1980s. The crisis occurred due to the liberal lending by the international financial institutions to the Latin American countries and consequently the interest rate has been raised and as a result these countries found it difficult to service their debt. The crisis, as it seems from the above discussions was the result of lack of visionary steps taken by the government of Latin American countries and also by the financial institutions. So, the lessons from the crisis is that while making the lending and borrowing decisions, both the parties should adopt the judicious approach and think about the future debt service capacity of the borrower and not only concentrate on the current debt service capacity of the borrowers. If these things are followed then only the financial crisis of this kind in the future can be prevented.

4 US Savings and Loan Crisis

United States of America during the period of 1980s and 1990s faced a unique kind of financial Crisis which is commonly known as the *Savings and Loan Crisis or* also commonly referred to as the *SandL crisis*. The crisis has taken place mainly because of the failures of 747 numbers of savings and loan associations (SandLs) in the United States. The ultimate cost of the crisis was estimated to have totaled around $ 160.1 billion out of which about $ 124.6 billion of which was directly paid for by the U.S. government—that is, the U.S. taxpayer, either directly or through

Overview of the Chapter

The S & L Crisis of the USA was occurred in the 1980s and 1990s. It was the failure of the savings and loan associations in USA. The present chapter describes the following items related to the S & L Crisis:

- The Background of the Crisis
- Causes of Crisis
- Failure of Government Machineries
- Cases of major S & L Associations failure
- Financial Institutions Reforms, Recovery and Enforcement Act of 1989
- Consequences
- Conclusion

charges on their savings and loan accounts which contributed to the large budget deficits of the early 1990s.

The contributing cause of the crisis was the slowdown in the finance industry and the real estate market. The United States has achieved the lowest number of new homes constructed per year since the World War II. Between 1986 and 1991, it dropped from 1.8 million to 1 million.

INTRODUCTION

In USA, the Savings and loan associations (also known as SandLs or thrifts) have existed since the 1800s. They originally served as community-based institutions for savings and mortgages. In the United States, SandLs were tightly regulated until the late 1970s. For example, there was a ceiling on the interest rates they could offer to depositors.

In the 1970s, many banks, but more particularly S and Ls, were experiencing a significant outflow of cash from low-interest rate deposits, as interest rates were driven up by the high inflation rate of the late 1970s and the depositors used to move their money to the new high-interest money market funds. At the same time, the institutions had much of their money tied up in long-term mortgage loans at fixed interest rates. Since the market interest rates were rising, the value of properties started falling. So, the value of the mortgaged properties which were tied with these financial institutions was worth far less than face value. That is, to sell a 5 percent mortgage to pay requests from depositors for their funds in a market asking 10 percent, a savings and loan would have to discount its asking price on the mortgage. This meant that the value of these loans, which were the institutions assets, was less than the deposits used to make them, and the savings and loan's net worth was being eroded.

Under financial institution regulation, which had its roots in the Civil War era, federally chartered SandLs were only allowed to make a narrowly limited range of loan types. Of Late in the administration of President Jimmy Carter, the caps were lifted on the interest rates and the amounts insured per account to $ 100,000. In addition to raising the amounts covered by insurance, the amount of the accounts that would be repaid was increased from 70 percent to 100 percent. Increasing Federal Savings and Loan Insurance Corporation (FSLIC) coverage also permitted managers to take more risk to try to work their way out of insolvency so the government would not have to take over an institution.

Carter left office in January 1981, the year in which 3,300 out of 3,800 SandLs lost money. In 1982 under Ronald Reagan became the president. At that time, the combined tangible net capital of the industry was $ 4 billion. The chartering of federally regulated SandLs accelerated rapidly with the Garn-St. Germain Depository Institutions Act of 1982, which was designed to make SandLs more competitive and more solvent. SandLs could now pay higher market rates for deposits, borrow money from the Federal Reserve, make commercial loans, and issue credit cards. They were also allowed to take an ownership position in the real estate and other projects to which they made loans and they began to rely on brokered funds to a considerable extent. This was a departure from their original mission of providing savings and mortgages.

CAUSES OF THE CRISIS

Tax Reform Act of 1986

The Tax Reform Act of 1986 removed many tax shelters; especially for real estate investments as a result there was a significant decrease in the value of many such investments which had been held more for their tax-advantaged status rather than for their inherent profitability. This contributed to the end of the real estate boom of the early 80s to mid-'80s and facilitated the Savings and Loan crisis. Prior to 1986, most of the real estate investment was done by passive investors. It was common for syndicates of investors to pool their resources in order to invest in property, whether it is commercial or residential. They would then hire management companies to run the operation. Tax Reform Act of 1986, reduced the value of these investments by limiting the extent to which losses associated with them could be deducted from the investor's gross income. This, in turn, encouraged the holders of loss-generating properties to try and unload them, which contributed further to the problem of sinking real estate values. This was an instance to show that the turmoil and repositioning in real estate markets was caused not by changes in market conditions but by the change in the tax laws of the country.

Deregulation

The deregulation of SandLs gave those many of the capabilities of banks; however, the regulations of the banks were not applicable on them. Savings and loan associations could choose to be under either a state or a federal charter. Immediately after deregulation of the federally chartered thrifts, state-chartered thrifts rushed to become federally chartered, because of the advantages associated with a federal charter. In response, states such as California and Texas changed their regulations so to be similar to federal regulations.

Imprudent Real Estate Lending

In an effort to take advantage of the real estate boom and high interest rates of the late 1970s and early 1980s, many SandLs lent far more money than was prudent, and to risky ventures which many SandLs were not qualified to assess. L. William Seidman, former chairman of both the Federal Deposit Insurance Corporation (FDIC) and the Resolution Trust Corporation, stated, "The banking problems of the '80s and '90s came primarily, but not exclusively, from unsound real estate lending."

Keeping Insolvent S and Ls Open

Whereas insolvent banks in the United States were typically detected and shut down quickly by bank regulators, Congress sought to change regulatory rules so SandLs would not have to acknowledge insolvency and the Federal Home Loan Bank Board (FHLBB) would not have to close them down.

Brokered Deposits

One of the most important contributors to the problem was deposit brokerage. Deposit brokers, somewhat like stockbrokers, are paid a commission by the customer to find the best certificate of deposit (CD) rates and place their customers' money in those CDs. These CDs, however, are usually short-term. Previously, banks and thrifts could only have five percent of their deposits as brokered deposits; but later on in order to get more and more deposits this limit was lifted. As a result, even small one-branch thrift could then attract a large number of deposits simply by offering the highest rate of commission. For the S and Ls, to make money off this expensive money, they had to lend at even higher rates, meaning that it had to make more, riskier investments. This system was made even more damaging when certain deposit brokers instituted a scam known as "linked financing". In "linked financing", a deposit broker would approach a thrift and say he would steer a large amount of deposits to that thrift if the thrift would lend certain people money (the people, however, were paid a fee to apply for the loans and told to give the loan proceeds to the deposit broker). This caused the thrifts to be tricked into taking on bad loans. Michael Milken of Drexel, Burnham and Lambert packaged brokered funds for several SandLs on the condition that the institutions would invest in the junk bonds of his clients.

End of Inflation

Another factor was the efforts of the Federal Reserve to bring inflation out of the economy, marked by Paul Volcker's speech of October 6, 1979, with a series of rises in short-term interest rates. This led to increases in the short-term cost of funding to be higher than the return on portfolios of mortgage loans, a large proportion of which may have been fixed rate mortgages (a problem that is known as an asset-liability mismatch). This effort failed and interest rates continued to skyrocket, placing even more pressure on SandLs as the 1980s dawned and led to increased focus on high interest-rate transactions. Zvi Bodie, professor of finance and economics at Boston University School of Management, writing in the St. Louis Federal Reserve *Review* wrote, "asset-liability mismatch was a principal cause of the Savings and Loan Crisis".

Major Causes According to United States League of Savings Institutions

According to the United States League of Savings Institutions the detailed summary of the major causes for losses that hurt the savings and loan business in the 1980s:

1. Lack of net worth for many institutions as they entered the '80s, and a wholly inadequate net worth regulation.
2. Decline in the effectiveness of regulation in preserving the spread between the cost of money and the rate of return on assets, basically stemming from inflation and the accompanying increase in market interest rates.
3. Absence of an ability to vary the return on assets with increases in the rate of interest required to be paid for deposits.
4. Increased competition on the deposit gathering and mortgage origination sides of the business, with a sudden burst of new technology making possible a whole new way of conducting financial institutions generally and the mortgage business specifically.
5. Savings and Loans gained a wide range of new investment powers with the passage of the Depository Institutions Deregulation and Monetary Control Act and the Garn-St. Germain Depository Institutions Act. A number of states also passed legislation that similarly increased investment options. These introduced new risks and speculative opportunities which were difficult to administer. In many instances management lacked the ability or experience to evaluate them, or to administer large volumes of non-residential construction loans.
6. Elimination of regulations initially designed to prevent lending excesses and minimize failures. Regulatory relaxation permitted lending, directly and through participations, in distant loan markets on the promise of high returns. Lenders, however, were not familiar with these distant markets. It also permitted associations to participate extensively in speculative

construction activities with builders and developers who had little or no financial stake in the projects.

7. Fraud and insider transaction abuses were the principal cause for some 20% of savings and loan failures the past three years and a greater percentage of the dollar losses borne by the Federal Savings and Loan Insurance Corporation (FSLIC).
8. A new type and generation of opportunistic savings and loan executives and owners—some of whom operated in a fraudulent manner—whose takeover of many institutions was facilitated by a change in FSLIC rules reducing the minimum number of stockholders of an insured association from 400 to one.
9. Dereliction of duty on the part of the board of directors of some savings associations. This permitted management to make uncontrolled use of some new operating authority, while directors failed to control expenses and prohibit obvious conflict of interest situations.
10. A virtual end of inflation in the American economy, together with overbuilding in multifamily, condominium type residences and in commercial real estate in many cities. In addition, real estate values collapsed in the energy states—Texas, Louisiana, Oklahoma particularly due to falling oil prices—and weakness occurred in the mining and agricultural sectors of the economy.
11. Pressures felt by the management of many associations to restore net worth ratios. Anxious to improve earnings, they departed from their traditional lending practices into credits and markets involving higher risks, but with which they had little experience.
12. The lack of appropriate, accurate, and effective evaluations of the savings and loan business by public accounting firms, security analysts, and the financial community.
13. Organizational structure and supervisory laws, adequate for policing and controlling the business in

the protected environment of the 1960s and 1970s, resulted in fatal delays and indecision in the examination/supervision process in the 1980s.

14. Federal and state examination and supervisory staffs insufficient in number, experience, or ability to deal with the new world of savings and loan operations.
15. The inability or unwillingness of the Bank Board and its legal and supervisory staff to deal with problem institutions in a timely manner. Many institutions, which ultimately closed with big losses, were known problem cases for a year or more. Often, it appeared, political considerations delayed necessary supervisory action.

Failures of the Government Machineries

In 1980, the US Congress has granted all the savings and loan associations, the power to make consumer and commercial loans and to issue transaction accounts. Designed to help the thrift industry retain its deposit base and to improve its profitability, the Depository Institutions Deregulation and Monetary Control Act (DIDMCA) of 1980 allowed thrifts to make consumer loans up to 20 percent of their assets, issue credit cards, accept negotiable order of withdrawal (NOW) accounts from individuals and non-profit organizations, and invest up to 20 percent of their assets in commercial real estate loans.

The damage to S and L operations led Congress pass a bill in September 1981 allowing S and Ls to sell their mortgage loans and use the cash generated to seek better returns; the losses created by the sales were to be amortized over the life of the loan, and any losses could also be offset against taxes paid over the preceding 10 years. This all made S and Ls eager to sell their loans. The buyers—major Wall Street firms—were quick to take advantage of the S and Ls' lack of expertise, buying at 60%-90% of value and then transforming the loans by bundling them as, effectively, government-backed bonds (by virtue of Ginnie Mae, Freddie Mac, or Fannie Mae guarantees). SandLs were one group buying these bonds, holding $ 150 billion by 1986, and being charged substantial fees for the transactions.

In 1982, the Garn-St Germain Depository Institutions Act was passed and increased the proportion of assets that thrifts could hold in consumer and commercial real estate loans and allowed thrifts to invest 5 percent of their assets in commercial loans until January 1, 1984, when this percentage increased to 10 percent.

A large number of S and L customers' defaults and bankruptcies ensued, and the S and Ls that had overextended themselves were forced into insolvency proceedings themselves.

The U.S. government agency FSLIC, which at the time insured S and L accounts in the same way the Federal Deposit Insurance Corporation insures commercial bank accounts, then had to repay all the depositors whose money was lost. From 1986 to 1989, FSLIC closed or otherwise resolved 296 institutions with total assets of $ 125 billion. An even more traumatic period followed, with the creation of the Resolution Trust Corporation in 1989 and that agency's resolution by mid-1995 of an additional 747 thrifts.

A Federal Reserve Bank panel stated the resulting taxpayer bailout ended up being even larger than it would have been because moral hazard and adverse selection incentives that compounded the system's losses.

There also were state-chartered SandLs that failed. Some state insurance funds failed, requiring state taxpayer bailouts.

CAUSES OF FAILURE OF SOME IMPORTANT S AND Ls

Home State Savings Bank of Cincinnati

In March 1985, it came to public knowledge that the large Cincinnati, Ohio-based Home State Savings Bank was about to collapse. Ohio Gov. Dick Celeste declared a bank holiday in the state as Home State depositors lined up in a "run" on the bank's branches to withdraw their deposits. Celeste ordered the closure of all the state's SandLs. Only those that were able to qualify for membership in the Federal Deposit Insurance Corporation were allowed to reopen. Claims by Ohio S and L depositors drained the state's deposit insurance funds. A similar event took place in Maryland.

Lincoln Savings and Loan

The Lincoln S and L led to the Keating five political scandals, in which five U.S. senators were implicated in an influence-peddling scheme. It was named for Charles Keating, who headed Lincoln Savings and made $ 300,000 as political contributions to them in the 1980s. Three of those senators–Alan Cranston (D-CA), Don Riegle (D-MI), and Dennis DeConcini (D-AZ)—found their political careers cut short as a result. Two others–John Glenn (D-OH) and John McCain (R-AZ)—were rebuked by the Senate Ethics Committee for exercising "poor judgment" for intervening with the federal regulators on behalf of Keating.

Silverado Savings and Loan

Silverado Savings and Loan collapsed in 1988, costing taxpayers $ 1.3 billion. Neil Bush, son of then Vice-President of the United States George H.W. Bush, was Director of Silverado at the time. Neil Bush was accused of giving himself a loan from Silverado, but he denied all wrongdoing.

The US Office of Thrift Supervision investigated Silverado's failure and determined that Neil Bush had engaged in numerous "breaches of his fiduciary duties involving multiple conflicts of interest." Although Bush was not indicted on criminal charges, a civil action was brought against him and the other Silverado directors by the Federal Deposit Insurance Corporation; it was eventually settled out of court, with Bush paying $ 50,000 as part of the settlement as was reported by the *Washington Post* reported.

As a director of a failing thrift, Bush voted to approve $ 100 million in what were ultimately bad loans to two of his business partners. And in voting for the loans, he failed to inform fellow board members at Silverado Savings and Loan that the loan applicants were his business partners.

Neil Bush paid a $ 50,000 fine and was banned from banking activities for his role in taking down Silverado, which cost taxpayers $ 1.3 billion. A Resolution Trust Corporation Suit against Bush and other officers of Silverado was settled in 1991 for $ 26.5 million.

FINANCIAL INSTITUTIONS REFORMS, RECOVERY AND ENFORCEMENT

As a result, the Financial Institutions Reform, Recovery, and Enforcement Act of 1989 (FIRREA) dramatically changed the savings and loan industry and its federal regulation. The highlights of the legislation, signed into law August 9, 1989, were:

1. The Federal Home Loan Bank Board (FHLBB) and the Federal Savings and Loan Insurance Corporation (FSLIC) were abolished.
2. The Office of Thrift Supervision (OTS), a bureau of the Treasury Department, was created to charter, regulate, examine, and supervise savings institutions.
3. The Federal Housing Finance Board (FHFB) was created as an independent agency to oversee the 12 federal home loan banks (also called district banks).
4. The Savings Association Insurance Fund (SAIF) replaced the FSLIC as an ongoing insurance fund for thrift institutions (like the FDIC, the FSLIC was a permanent corporation that insured savings and loan accounts up to $ 100,000). SAIF is administered by the Federal Deposit Insurance Corp.
5. The Resolution Trust Corporation (RTC) was established to dispose of failed thrift institutions taken over by regulators after January 1, 1989. The RTC will make insured deposits at those institutions available to their customers.
6. FIRREA gives both Freddie Mac and Fannie Mae additional responsibility to support mortgages for low- and moderate-income families.

CONSEQUENCES

Although not part of the savings and loan crisis, many other banks failed. Between 1980 and 1994 more than 1,600 banks insured by the Federal Deposit Insurance Corporation (FDIC) were closed or received FDIC financial assistance.

From 1986 to 1995, the number of US federally insured savings and loans in the United States declined from 3,234 to 1,645. This was primarily, but not exclusively, due to unsound real estate lending.

The market share of SandLs for single family mortgage loans went from 53% in 1975 to 30% in 1990. U.S. General Accounting Office estimated cost of the crisis to around USD $ 160.1 billion, about $ 124.6 billion of which was directly paid for by the U.S. government from 1986 to 1996. That figure does not include thrift insurance funds used before 1986 or after 1996. It also does not include state run thrift insurance funds or state bailouts.

The U.S. government ultimately appropriated 105 billion dollars to resolve the crisis. After banks repaid loans through various procedures, there was a net loss to taxpayers of approximately $ 124 billion dollars by the end of 1999.

Some commentators believe that a taxpayer-funded government bailout related to mortgages during the savings and loan crisis may have created a moral hazard and acted as encouragement to lenders to make similar higher risk loans during the 2007 sub-prime mortgage financial crisis.

CONCLUSION

The objective of the chapter was to present before the readers the situation in brief about the saving and loan crisis of the United States. Thus, it is seen that overall the cause of the crisis was partly the unwise and unforesighted decisions of the government and partly the S and Ls of the USA. In a hurry to make maximum profit they forgotten the fundamentals of the business and get involved in some of the unsound business practices which ultimately led to their failures causing the wastages to the taxpayers money in the form of several incentives from the government and bailout packages.

5 Japanese Asset Price Bubble

Overview of the Chapter

The Economic Crisis has also hit Japan in the year 1986 to 1990. The present chapter highlights about the burst of the Japanese Asset Price Bubble. The main Contents of the chapter are:

- Asset Price Bubble Since 1980s
- Effect on Financial and Macro-economic Stability
- Implications of Bubble
- Conclusion

Japan is one of the leading economies of the Asia. But Japan has also faced financial crisis during the period 1986 to 1990. The crisis was basically due to the burst of the asset price bubble in Japan. The *Japanese asset price bubble* was an economic bubble in Japan from 1986 to 1990, in which real estate and stock prices greatly inflated. The bubble's collapse lasted for more than a decade with stock prices bottoming in 2003, until hitting an even lower low in 2008 amidst a global recession. This shows that how bursting of the bubble can play an important role in the economic fluctuations. This experience clearly indicates that both financial and macroeconomic instability is closely related to large fluctuations in asset prices, and raises the question of what is the appropriate way to treat asset prices in macroeconomic policy-making.

It should be noted regarding Japan's experience is that enthusiasm of market participants with not consistent projection of fundamentals had contributed largely to maintaining temporarily high asset prices at that time. Such enthusiasm is often called euphoria, which is excessively optimistic but unfounded expectations for the long-term economic performance last for several years and then burst.

In this context, it is crucial to accurately analyze what asset price fluctuations imply and to accurately evaluate how expectations illustrated in such fluctuations are sustainable. In retrospect, prevailing expectations during Japan's late 1980s was that Japan was entering a new era of economic development corresponding to optimistic expectations for potential growth. It was thus excessive optimism rather than consistent projection of fundamentals that mainly supported temporarily high asset prices. As a result, increase in asset prices during this period failed to deliver a sufficient clue to assess whether such increase was consequence of an advent of a new economy or just euphoria.

ASSET PRICE BUBBLE SINCE 1980s

Japan's Asset Price Fluctuations in the Post-World War II Period

Japan has experienced three major boom-bust cycles in asset prices in the postwar period. These are:

(1) The *Iwato* boom in the second half of the 1950s;
(2) The boom of Prime Minister Tanaka's 'remodeling the Japanese archipelago' project; and
(3) The *Heisei* boom in the late 1980s to early 1990s.

First, at the time of the *Iwato* boom, when Japan's economy entered the so called 'high-economic-growth-period,' asset prices increased rapidly, reflecting an improvement in fundamentals due to technological innovation. The real economic growth rate exceeded 10 percent per annum, driven mainly by investment demand which is due to technological innovation that replaced the post World War II reconstruction demand. On the price front, consumer prices rose while wholesale prices remained generally stable, thus leading to the so-called 'productivity-difference-inflation.'

Second, during the period from the 'remodeling the Japanese archipelago' boom to the first oil crisis, asset prices first increased and then the general price level sharply rose due to the excessively high growth of money stock and oil price hikes stemming from the first oil crisis. In the mean time, real economic growth rapidly declined marking an end to the high economic growth period.

Third, in the *Heisei* boom, asset prices increased dramatically under long lasting economic growth and stable inflation. Okina, Shirakawa, and Shiratsuka (2000) define the 'bubble period' as the period from 1987 to 1990, from the viewpoint of coexistence of three factors of the bubble economy, that is, a marked increase in asset prices, an expansion of monetary aggregates and credit, and an over-heating of economic activity. The phenomena particular to this period were stable CPI inflation parallel with the expansion of asset prices and long adjustment period after the peaking of asset prices.

The decline in asset prices was initially regarded as the bursting of asset price bubble, and the amplifying factor of a business cycle. Although the importance of cyclical aspects cannot be denied, further declines in asset prices after the mid-1990s seem to reflect the downward shift in trend growth rate beyond the boom-and-bust cycle of the asset price bubble.

Mechanism Behind the Emergence and Expansion of the Bubble

Focusing on the third episode above, the bubble was generated by the complex interaction of various factors as a process of 'intensified bullish expectations'. The intensified bullish expectations are clearly observed in the increased equity yield spread during the period form the late 1980s to the early 1990s. As reported by Okina, Shirakawa, and Shiratsuka (2000), the expected growth rate of nominal GDP computed from the equity yield spread in 1990 is as high as 8 percentage points with the standard assumption based on the discount factor. However, in view of the low inflation at the time, it is almost impossible to believe that the potential growth rate of nominal GDP was close to 8%. Hence, it would be more natural to infer that the high level of the yield spread in 1990 reflected the intensification of bullish expectations, which are unsustainable in the long run. The intensified bullish expectations were surely grounded in several factors intertwined with each other. The factors below are often pointed out as behind the emergence and expansion of the bubble:

- Aggressive behaviour of financial institutions.
- Progress of financial deregulation
- Inadequate risk management on the part of financial institutions.
- Introduction of the capital accord.
- Protracted monetary easing.
- Taxation and regulations biased toward accelerating the rise in land prices.
- Overconfidence and euphoria.
- Over-concentration of economic functions on Tokyo, and Tokyo becoming an international financial center.

Focusing on monetary factors, it is important to note that widespread market expectations that the then low interest rates would continue for an extended period, in spite of clear signs of economic expansion. The movement of implied forward rates from 1987 through 1989 shows that the yield curve flattened while the official discount rate was maintained at a low level.

EFFECT ON FINANCIAL AND MACROECONOMIC STABILITY

In this section, the lessons of Japan's asset price bubbles in terms of financial and monetary stability have been examined. Three points have been considered below:

(i) build-up of risks during the period of bubble expansion;
(ii) vulnerability of the bank-based financial system; and
(iii) weakened effects of monetary easing.

Build-up of Risks during the Period of Bubble Expansion

The first lesson is that risks of financial and macroeconomic instability are built up during asset price booms and such risks are materialized as an aftermath of asset price declines and recessions. In light of Japan's experience, it seems to be a characteristic that effects of a bubble are asymmetrically larger in the bursting period than in the expansion period. A rise and fall in asset prices, which contain an element of a bubble, influence real economic activity mainly through two routes: (i) on consumption through the wealth effect, and (ii) on investment through a change in external finance premium due to changes in collateral and net asset values. As far as asset prices are rising, they influence the economy in a favorable way and the adverse effects are not thoroughly recognized. However, once the economy enters a downturn, the above favourable cycle reverses, thereby leading to a severe reaction. The harmful effects of a bubble will emerge, exerting stress on the real side of the economy and financial system due to an unexpected correction of asset prices. If intensified bullish expectations which previously supported the bubble are left unchecked, expansion and subsequent bursting of the bubble will become bigger, affecting the real economy directly or, by damaging the financial system, indirectly. Looking at the land price problem from the viewpoint of the stability of the financial system, it was the risk brought about by the sharp rise in land prices and the concentration of credit in the real estate and related industries that were insufficiently perceived. During the bubble period, real estate was generally accepted as collateral. However, if the profitability of businesses financed by secured loans is closely related to collateral value, such loans become practically unsecured since profits and collateral value move in the same direction. In fact, Shimizu and Shiratsuka (2000) show a simple numerical exercise, based on an analytical framework of value at risk (VaR), enables us to sufficiently predict the magnitude of non-performing loans held by Japanese banks in the 1990s ('stress testing'). The exercise estimates the aggregate credit risk inherent in the loan portfolio of Japanese banks during the bubble period by assuming sufficiently prudent scenarios for the probability of bankruptcy, the concentration of credit and the future fluctuation of collateral prices.

Vulnerability of a Bank-based Financial System

The second lesson is that the vulnerability of Japan's banking system against very large and unexpected shocks increased significantly in the late 1980s. In a financial system, banks play a buffer role against short-term shocks by accumulating internal reserves when the economy is sound while absorbing losses stemming from firms' poor business performance or bankruptcy during recession. Even though some risks cannot be diversified only at a particular point in time, such risks can nevertheless be diversified over time. However, in order to achieve a more efficient allocation of risks in the economy, one needs not just markets for cross sectional risk sharing but a sufficient accumulation of reserves as a buffer for intertemporal risk smoothing. Such a risk smoothing function of the banking sector, however, is difficult to maintain under financial liberalization and more intense competition from financial markets. Intertemporal smoothing requires that investors accept lower returns than the market offers in some periods in order to get higher returns in others. Investors, however, would opt out of the banking system and invest in the financial markets, thereby deteriorating banks' internal reserves. As a result, a risk smoothing function is more easily and suddenly lost than before, once the economy encounters a shock that erodes banks' net capital to the extent it threatens their soundness. In fact, during the bubble era, gradual financial deregulation led to undermining the profitability of the banking sector in Japan, thereby deteriorating the risk smoothing function in the banking sector. Against the background of financial liberalization, fund-raising by major firms had been rapidly liberalized since around 1980, while banks were only allowed to enter the securities business gradually. Thus banks were very concerned that major firms would become less dependent on them for funding. In the meantime, since interest rates on deposits had gradually been liberalized, banks forwent the rent stemming from accepting deposits with regulated interest rates and were inclined to aggressively extend loans to small and medium-sized enterprises against real estate collateral as well as real state related loans at low interest rates. In retrospect, such aggressive lending at low interest rates seemed to have been pursued by financial institutions taking excessive risks compared with their profit outlook. In this connection, two points should be also noted. First, a bank-based financial system, like Japan has, absorbs more risks from households than a market based financial system does. Risk allocation in the economy thus should have been very different, if the economy had a market-based financial system even under a similar course of financial and economic development. Second, a bank-based financial system tends to magnify the adverse effects of the bursting of bubbles on real economic activity due to the longer time lag until their materialization.

Weakened Effects of Monetary Easing

The third lesson is that the effectiveness of the central bank's monetary easing is substantially counteracted when the financial system carries problems stemming from the bursting of a bubble. Although it is difficult to give a direct answer to the above question, the quantitative growth of financial indicators suggests that the current monetary easing phase is different and unusual compared with past easing phases. First, on a quantitative aspect, monetary base (which are the liabilities of the Bank of Japan) had been showing marked growth, money supply (M2+CDs) has been growing at a low rate and bank loans have been declining. Second, on fund allocation front, loans to manufacturing industries, which are believed to carry relatively high profitability, had declined throughout the 1990s; loans to the real estate industry followed an increasing trend until 1998. The above observation suggests the possibility of two mechanisms. First, an increase in non-performing loans erodes the net capital of financial institutions, resulting in a decline in risk-taking ability (credit crunch). Second, even though firms become unprofitable, financial institutions continue lending to them to prevent losses from materializing (forbearance lending). Under such circumstances, loans to unprofitable firms become fixed and funds are not channeled to growing firms, holding down economic activity. Moreover, monetary easing alone was unable to offset amplified shocks beyond the boom-bust cycle of asset price fluctuations. Nagahata and Sekine (2002) showed that the positive impacts of lowering interest rates worked, although such easing impacts were offset by the negative impacts of deteriorated balance sheet conditions at the firms as well as banks. As a related issue, it should be stressed that, once a financial system tumbles into a critical situation, the boundary between monetary and prudential policies becomes extremely ambiguous. Money market operations under financial crises have a larger burden of liquidity management in various markets, in addition to a standard role as a starting point of monetary policy transmission. More precisely, during financial crises, financially stressed banks tend to have serious difficulties not only with lending, but also arbitraging and dealing. This hampers the transmission mechanism from the policy-targeted rate to longer-term rates, resulting in segmentation among various financial markets. Thus, it could be extremely important for a central bank to intervene in various financial markets to fix segmented markets, thereby restoring market liquidity and the proper transmission mechanism.

IMPLICATIONS OF THE BUBBLE

Taylor Rule

Taylor rule has an important implication over the central bank to deal with the asset price fluctuations in a pre-emptive manner. In the most basic formulation, the Taylor rule considers that the operational target level of the interest rate should be determined according to the divergence of the inflation rate and output gap from their equilibrium level. The standard interpretation of the Taylor rule is that a central bank has two objectives on the level of economic activity, inflation and output gap, whose relative importance is evaluated by the coefficients of each objective variable. However, if the output gap as a proxy of future inflationary pressure is regarded, the

Taylor rule can be interpreted as a rule that responds to current and future price developments. Within the framework of the Taylor rule, Bernanke and Gertler (1999) argue that it is possible for a central bank to deal with potential inflationary pressure in a pre-emptive manner. This is because effects of asset price fluctuations are included in changes in the current output gap. They present simulation results that the BOJ should have been able to achieve better performance if it had pursued a Taylor-type rule that discards asset price fluctuations. In fact, their policy rule points the need for rapid tightening of raising the interest rate from 4 to 8 percent in 1988, despite of focusing only on the inflation and output gap. Okina and Shiratsuka (2002, 2003) point out, however, that Bernanke and Gertler's (1999) conclusion depends crucially on their treatment of the consumption tax in compiling a core inflation rate. They show that the spike of the policy rate in 1998, observed in Bernanke and Gertler (1999), disappears when they adjust for the introduction of the consumption tax (3 percent) in April 1989. They concludes that it was difficult for the BOJ to pursuit the rapid monetary tightening in 1988 as Bernanke and Gertler pointed, if one consider that onetime price increases induced by an introduction of the consumption tax should not be offset by monetary tightening.

Output Gap and Trend Growth

Given the above argument on the Taylor rule, two components of the Taylor rule, output gap and inflation have been examined. The assessment of potential GDP differed whether one adopted the optimistic expectations at the time or accepted the potential growth rate based on the benefit of hindsight that such expectations were nothing more than euphoria. In the case of euphoria, the perceived potential output path shifts upward as economic expansion prolongs, resulting in the underestimation of inflationary pressure in view of the output gap. On the contrary, in the case of a rational bubble, an output gap is assessed based on recognition that the potential output path remains unchanged. Thus, market participants correctly recognize fundamental values of asset prices as well as the sustainability of currently overvalued asset prices, which leads to the same judgement as one reaches, with the benefit of hindsight, that asset price increase was totally the result of euphoria. What typically shows this point is the evaluation of the real GDP growth path on a real-time basis. 1987 is the bottom of the yen appreciation recession prior to the bubble period. At this point, when one plots a linear trend line from 1977 to 1987, it approximately corresponds to a trend of 3.5-percent growth. However, from 1987 to mid-1991, real GDP expanded following a trend line of 5-percent growth. Given the above argument, it is deemed crucial that the risk of committing type II error increases, as economic expansion prolongs.

Inflation

At the time of the bubble period, the CPI was extremely stable until around 1987, but started to rise gradually in 1988. The year-on-year increase in the CPI, adjusted for the impact of consumption tax, continued to rise after April 1989, and it reached 2% in April 1990 and 3% in November 1990. From the viewpoint of 'measured price stability,' two evaluations are possible: (1) prices eventually rose substantially toward the end of the bubble period, compared with the recent level of inflation; and (2) price stability had not been undermined in comparison with the figure before the bubble period. The difference between the two evaluations, so to speak, boils down to the question of what can be regarded as a tolerable rate of inflation. There can be a variety of answers to this question. From the viewpoint of 'sustainable price stability,' however, it can be seen that Japan's economy experienced deflation as a result of the emergence of the bubble economy in the second half of the 1980s. In other words, the experience of the bubble period seems to suggest the importance of "the sustainability of price stability over a fairly long period."

Money Supply and Credit

During the bubble period, the large increase in money supply and credit also signaled the need for an early increase in interest rates. In fact, while the BOJ expressed concern over the increase in money supply from a relatively early stage, such concern, however, turned out not to be taken seriously. The major reason for this was lack of a common understanding, including on the part of the BOJ, as to what kind of problems might be occasioned by the massive expansion of money supply and credit. At that time, concern over the large increase in money supply was mainly based on the view that such an increase would eventually result in inflation. However, prices did not rise even though money supply increased. As a result, it was widely argued that the statistical relationship between money supply and prices had become unstable and this argument gradually prevailed. In addition, the on-going deregulation of deposit interest rates was often mentioned as a reason for the statistical instability. Based on Japan's experience, when money supply and credit show a very large upswing, we should pay close attention to such movements in the conduct of monetary policy on the presumption that such large fluctuations may indicate the possibility of undesirable development in economic activity.

CONCLUSION

This Chapter has reviewed the implications of asset price fluctuations on financial and macroeconomic stability in Japan in the late 1980s. A critical point is that Japan's asset price bubble was based on excessively optimistic expectations with respect to the future, which might be described as euphoria with the benefit of hindsight, rather than a rational bubble. Under continued price stability, the perceived potential output path shifted upward as economic expansion prolonged, resulting in the emergence of euphoria and underestimation of inflationary pressure in view of the output gap. However, the increase in asset prices during this period also failed to deliver a sufficient clue to assess whether such increase was the consequence of the advent of a new economy or just euphoria. After all, policy-makers are unlikely to take an appropriate policy response without evaluating whether expectations for a new stage of development induced by asset price hikes are euphoric or not, and forecast a correct path for the potential growth rate. In so doing, it is deemed important to assess financial and macroeconomic stability from the viewpoints of sustainability. It should be noted, however, that no rules exist regarding how to accurately recognize the risk profiles in the economy.

6 European Currency Crisis

> **Overview of the Chapter**
>
> In the current chapter the Currency Crisis of the European countries particularly of the Britain has been discussed. The following things have been included in the chapter:
>
> - Prelude of the Crisis
> - The Activities of the Currency Traders
> - Aftermath the Crisis
> - Conclusion

A unique kind of crisis has been witnessed by the Britain in 1992. In British politics and economics, *Black Wednesday* refers to the events of 16 September, 1992 when the Conservative government was forced to withdraw the pound from the European Exchange Rate Mechanism (ERM) after they were unable to keep Sterling above its agreed lower limit. The most high profile of the currency market investors, George Soros, made over US $ 1 billion profit by shorting the sterling. In 1997 the UK Treasury estimated the cost of Black Wednesday at h3.4 billion.

The trading losses in August and September were estimated at £ 800 m, but the main loss to taxpayers arose because the devaluation could have made them a profit. The news papers show that if the government had maintained

$ 24 bn foreign currency reserves and the pound had fallen by the same amount, the UK would have made a £ 2.4 bn profit on sterling's devaluation. Newspapers also revealed that the Treasury spent £ 27 bn of reserves in propping up the pound.

INTRODUCTION TO THE CRISIS

When the ERM was set up in 1979, Britain declined to join. This was a controversial decision as the Chancellor of the Exchequer Geoffrey Howe, despite his economically dry credentials, was a convinced pro-European. His successor Nigel Lawson was also a believer in a fixed exchange rate, and although he was a mild Eurosceptic he admired the low inflationary record of West Germany, attributing it to the strength of the Deutsche Mark and the management of the Bundesbank. Thus although Britain had not joined the ERM, from early 1987 to March 1988 the Treasury followed a semi-official policy of 'shadowing' the Deutsche Mark.

UK fiscal policy at the time was lax. Yet interest rates were set at relatively low rates and the risk of future inflation only appeared to be a secondary consideration in retrospect. Matters came to a head in a clash between Margaret Thatcher's economic advisor Alan Walters and Nigel Lawson, when Walters claimed that the Exchange Rate Mechanism was "half baked". This led to Lawson resigning as chancellor to be replaced by his old protégé John Major, who, with Douglas Hurd, the then Foreign Secretary, pressured Margaret Thatcher to sign Britain up to the ERM in October 1990, effectively guaranteeing that the British Government would follow an economic and monetary policy that would prevent the exchange rate between the pound and other member currencies from fluctuating by more than 6%. The pound entered the mechanism at DM 2.95 to the pound. Hence, if the exchange rate ever neared the bottom of its permitted range, DM 2.778, the government would be obliged to intervene. With UK inflation at three times of the inflation rate of Germany's; interest rates at 15% and the "Lawson Boom" about to bust, the conditions for joining the ERM were not favourable at that time.

From the beginning of the 1990s, High German interest rates, set by the Bundesbank to counteract inflationary effects related to excess expenditure on German reunification, caused significant stress across the whole of the ERM. The UK and Italy had additional difficulties with their double digit deficits, while the UK was also hurt by the rapid depreciation of the US Dollar because it was a currency in which many British exports were priced during that time. Issues of national prestige and the commitment to a doctrine that the fixing of exchange rates within the ERM was a pathway to a single European currency inhibited the adjustment of exchange rates. In the wake of the rejection of the Maastricht Treaty by the Danish electorate in a referendum in the spring of 1992, and announcement that there would be a referendum in France as well, those ERM currencies that were trading close to the bottom of their ERM bands came under pressure from foreign exchange traders.

ACTIVITIES OF CURRENCY TRADERS

The UK's prime minister and cabinet members tried all day to prop up a sinking pound and withdrawal from the monetary system the country had joined two years prior was the last resort. Prime Minister Mr. John Major raised interest rates from 10 to 12 percent, then to 15, and he authorized the spending of billions of pounds to buy up the sterling being frantically sold on the currency markets. But the measures failed to prevent the pound falling lower than its minimum level in the ERM.

The Treasury took the decision to defend Sterling's position. It was believed that to devalue the currency would promote inflation. On 16 September, the British government announced a rise in the base interest rate from an already high 10 to 12 percent in order to tempt speculators to buy pounds. Despite this and a promise later by the government the same day to raise base rates again to 15 percent, dealers kept selling pounds, convinced that the government would not stick with its promise. By 1900 hrs that evening, Norman Lamont, then Chancellor, announced Britain would leave the ERM and rates would remain at the new level of 12 percent. It was later revealed that the decision to withdraw had been agreed at an emergency meeting during the day between Norman Lamont, Prime Minister John Major, Foreign Secretary Douglas Hurd, President of the Board of Trade Michael Heseltine and Home Secretary Kenneth Clarke (the latter three all being strong pro-Europeans as well as senior Cabinet Ministers), and that the interest rate hike to 15 percent had only been a temporary measure to prevent a rout in the pound that afternoon.

AFTERMATH THE CRISIS

Other ERM countries such as Italy, whose currencies had breached their bands during the day, returned to the system with broadened bands or with adjusted central parities. Even in this relaxed form, ERM-I proved vulnerable, and ten months later the rules were relaxed further to the point of imposing very little constraint on the domestic monetary policies of member states.

The interest rates in Germany and Britain have shoot up during that period in order to control inflation. The effect of the High German interest rates, and high British interest rates, had been arguably to put Britain into recession as large numbers of businesses failed and the housing market crashed. In his memoirs, Mr. John Major claimed that ERM membership had the beneficial effect of wringing inflation out of Britain's system.

Indeed the performance of the UK economy subsequent to the events of Black Wednesday has been significantly stronger than that of the Euro zone and, despite the damage caused to the economy in the short-term, many economists now use the term 'White Wednesday' to describe the day (a term originally coined by Euro-sceptics happy at the stalling of further European integration). Ironically, sterling subsequently rallied strongly during the autumn of 1996 and early 1997 back to the levels which had prevailed before Black Wednesday, and sterling's trade-weighted index remained stable at these levels until late 2006.

However, the reputation of the Conservatives for competent handling of the economy was shattered. The Conservatives had recently won the 1992 General Election, and the Gallup poll for September showed a 2.5% Conservative lead. By the October poll, following Black Wednesday, they had plunged from 43% voting intention to 29%, while Labour jumped into a lead which they held more-or-less unbroken (except for several brief periods such as during the 2000 Fuel Protests) until David Cameron became leader of the Conservative Party. It took 15 years for the Conservatives to regain the 42%+ popularity that are considered the minimum necessary for a Conservative general election victory. David Cameron, then just short of 26 years old and unknown to the public, was political advisor to Norman Lamont, the Chancellor of the Exchequer, during the problems of Black Wednesday, and can be spotted at Lamont's side in news film of Lamont's announcement of British withdrawal from the ERM that evening.

EU economists' analysis of this event concluded that stable exchange rates are the result, not the cause, of a common approach to economic management, resulting in the Stability and Growth Pact that underpins ERM II and subsequently the euro single currency.

The incident is also often cited as an example of how economic globalization—the increased transnational mobility of finance capital—undermines the ability of governments to influence economic trends affecting their citizens. This not only poses a challenge to national economies at large, but to longstanding traditions of liberal representative democracy which still rest on assumptions of high state autonomy from external factors beyond those that arises from its relative power position within the international order.

CONCLUSION

It is observed that the economic crisis occurred not only due to the crash of the stock markets or due to the heavy inflation or interest rates but also because of the policy of the government with regard to the exchange rate of its currency. The current chapter shows how the problem developed in Europe and particularly in Britain which was due to the exchange rate mechanism. Like other crisis this crisis was also due to the some of the mistakes made by the government and partly due to the psychology of the traders of the currencies. This crisis has an impact on the politics of the Britain along with the economy.

7 Mexican Peso Crisis

> **Overview of the Chapter**
>
> The economic crisis in Mexico was due to the sudden devaluation of the Mexican Peso. The details of the crisis are given in the current chapter. The chapter includes the following:
>
> - Causes of the Crisis
> - Financial Assistance Package by the US Government
> - Conclusion

There was an economic crisis in Mexico. It was during the year *1994*. The economic crisis in *Mexico is w*idely known as the *Mexican peso crisis*. It was triggered by the sudden devaluation of the Mexican peso in the early days of Ernesto Zedillo's presidency. The crisis is known in Spanish as *el error de diciembre—The December Mistake*— a term coined by the then ex-president *Carlos Salinas de Gortari*. The impact of the Mexican economic crisis on Southern Cone and Brazil was labeled the *Tequila Effect*

CAUSES OF THE CRISIS

While the crisis took place under President Ernesto Zedillo, the causes are usually attributed to Carlos Salinas de

Gortari's outgoing administration. Salinas de Gortari partially coined the term "December Mistake" when he referred to Zedillo's sudden reversal of the former administrative policies of tight currency controls, "a mistake." His government's currency policy put a strain on the nation's finances; despite some saying by some people that the economic bubble gave Mexico prosperity.

As in prior election cycles, a pre-election disposition to stimulate the economy happens. It is temporary and unsustainable. It ultimately led to post-election economic instability. There were concerns about the level and quality of credit extended by banks during the preceding low-interest rate period, as well as the standards for extending credit. The country's risk premium was also affected by an armed rebellion in Chiapas, causing investors to be worry of investing their money in an unstable region. The Mexican government's finances and cash availability were further hampered by two decades of increasing spending, debt loads. Mexico is an oil producing country and its economy is also dependent on oil export. The low oil prices during those times have worsened the situation. Its ability to absorb shocks was hampered by its commitments to finance past spending.

Economists Hufbauer and Schott (2005) from the Institute for International Economics have commented on the macroeconomic policy mistakes that precipitated the crisis. These are given as follows:

- 1994 was the last year of the *sexenio,* or 6-year administration of Carlos Salinas de Gortari who, following the PRI tradition on an election year, launched a high spending splurge and a high deficit.
- In order to finance the deficit (7% of GDP current account deficit), Salinas issued the *Tesobonos;* a type of debt instrument denominated in pesos but indexed to dollars.
- Mexico experienced lax banking or corrupt practices; moreover, some members of the Salinas family collected enormous illicit payoffs.
- The EZLN, an insurgent rebellion, officially declared war on the government on January 1, 1994; even

though the armed conflict ended two weeks later, the grievances and petitions remained a cause of concern, especially amongst some investors.

Macroeconomics 5th Edition by Mankiw explains the country-risk issues precipitating the crisis as follows:

- The EZLN's violent uprising in *Chiaps* in 1994 along with the assassination of Presidential candidate Luis Donaldo Colosio made the nation's political future look less certain to investors, who then started placing a larger risk premium on Mexican assets.
- Mexico had a fixed exchange rate system that accepted Pesos during the reaction of investors to a higher perceived country risk premium and paid out Dollars. However, Mexico lacked sufficient foreign reserves to maintain the fixed exchange rate and was running out of dollars at the end of 1994. The Peso then had to be allowed to devalue despite the government's previous assurances to the contrary, thereby scaring investors away and further raising its risk profile.
- When the government tried to roll over some of its debt that was coming due, investors were unwilling to buy the debt and default became one of few options.
- A crisis of confidence damaged the banking system which in turn fed a vicious cycle further affecting investor confidence.

All of the above concerns, along with increasing current account deficit fostered by consumer binding and government spending, caused alarm among those who bought the *Tesobonos*. The investors sold the *Tesobonos* rapidly, depleting the already low central bank reserves. Given the fact that it was an election year, whose outcome might have changed as a result of a pre-election-day economic downturn, Banco de México [Central Bank of Mexico] decided to buy Mexican Treasury Securities to maintain the monetary base, thus keeping the interest rates from rising. This caused an even bigger decline in the dollar reserves. However, nothing was done during the last 5 months of Salinas' administration. Some critics affirm this maintained Salinas' popularity, as he was seeking international support to become director general of the WTO. Zedillo took office on December 1, 1994.

A few days after a private meeting with major Mexican entrepreneurs, in which his administration asked them for their opinion of a planned devaluation; Zedillo announced his government would let the fixed rate band increase to 15 percent (up to 4 pesos per US dollar), by stopping the previous administration's measures to keep it at the previous fixed level. The government, being unable even to hold this line, decided to let it float.

While critics agree devaluation was necessary, some critics of Zedillo's incumbent 22-day-old administration argue that although economically coherent, the way it was handled was politically incorrect. They argue that many foreigners withdrew their investments, aggravating the situation. The peso crashed under a floating regime from four pesos per dollar to 7.2 peso per dollar. The United States intervened rapidly, first by buying pesos in the open market, and then by granting assistance in the form of $ 50 billion in loan guarantees. The dollar stabilized at the rate of 6 pesos per dollar. By 1996, the economy was growing (peaked at 7% growth in 1999). In 1997, Mexico repaid, ahead of schedule, all US Treasury loans.

FINANCIAL ASSISTANCE PACKAGE

A week of intense currency crisis stabilized only after US President Bill Clinton, in concert with international organizations, granted a $ 20 billion loan to Mexico. By extending loans to the Mexican government the Clinton administration stopped US banks collapsing as a result of the Mexican default. Thus US banks were protected from the effects of giving excessive loans to a poor creditor while the Mexican economy was saddled with further debt.

Loans and guarantees to Mexico totaled almost $ 50 billion, with the following contributions:

- The United States arranged currency swaps and loan guarantees with a $ 20 billion total value.
- The IMF promised an 18 month Stand-by Credit Agreement of around US $ 17.7 billion.
- The Bank for International Settlements offered a $ 10 billion line of credit.
- The Bank of Canada offered short-term swaps with a US dollar value of around one billion.

The United State's assistance was provided via the treasury's Exchange Stabilization Fund (ESF). This was slightly controversial, as President Clinton tried and failed to pass the Mexican Stabilization Act through Congress. However, use of the ESF allowed the provision of funds without the approval of the legislative branch. At the end of the crisis, the U.S. actually made a $ 500 million profit on the loans.

CONCLUSION

It can be concluded from the above discussion that the economic crisis in Mexico was because of the sudden devaluation of its currency called Peso. As a result the economy of the Mexico gets affected badly. Moreover, the amounts of debt over the country and the falling oil prices have added oil to the fire. Later on the US president Bill Clinton have interfered and provided help to the Mexico to save its economy. Finally Mexico was able to come out of the crisis and have repaid the foreign loans much ahead of the schedule.

8 Asian Financial Crisis

Overview of the Chapter

The present chapter deals with the economic crisis of Asia during the year 1997 onward. It was primarily a crisis generated due to the currency speculation and hence also called as the Asian Currency Crisis. The chapter highlights the following important headings:

- Causes of the Crisis
- The role of IMF
- IMF and High Interest Rates
- Thailand and the Crisis
- Indonesia and the Crisis
- South Korea and the Crisis
- Philippines and the Crisis
- Hong Kong and the Crisis
- Malaysia and the Crisis
- Singapore and the Crisis
- China and the Crisis
- US, Japan and the Crisis
- Consequences of the Crisis
- Conclusion

The *Asian Financial Crisis* was a period of financial crisis that gripped much of Asia beginning in July 1997, and raised fears of a worldwide economic melt-down.

The crisis started in Thailand. It was caused by the financial collapse of the Thai baht which was caused by the decision of the Thai government to float the baht, cutting its peg to the USD, after exhaustive efforts to support it in the face of a severe financial overextension that was in part real estate driven. At that time, Thailand had acquired a burden of foreign debt that made the country effectively bankrupt even before the collapse of its currency. As the crisis spread, most of Southeast Asia and Japan saw slumping currencies, devalued stock markets and other asset prices, and a precipitous rise in private debt.

Though there has been general agreement on the existence of a crisis and its consequences, what are less clear are the causes of the crisis, as well as its scope and resolution. Indonesia, South Korea and Thailand were the countries most affected by the crisis. Hong Kong, Malaysia, Laos and the Philippines were also hurt by the slump. The People's Republic of China, India, Taiwan, Singapore, Brunei and Vietnam were less affected, although all suffered from a loss of demand and confidence throughout the region.

Foreign debt-to-GDP ratios raised from 100% to 167% in the four large Asian economies, namely, Thailand, Indonesia, Malaysia, and South Korea in 1993-96, and then shot up beyond 180% during the worst of the crisis. In Korea, the ratios rose from 13%-21% and then as high as 40%, while the other Northern NICs (Newly Industrialized Countries) fared much better. Only in Thailand and Korea did debt service-to-exports ratios rise.

Although most of the governments of Asia had seemingly sound fiscal policies, the International Monetary Fund (IMF) stepped in to initiate a $ 40 billion program to stabilize the currencies of South Korea, Thailand, and Indonesia, economies particularly hard hit by the crisis. However, the efforts to stem a global economic crisis did little to stabilize the domestic situation in Indonesia. After 30 years in power, President Suharto was forced to step down in May 1998 in the wake of widespread rioting that followed sharp price increases caused by a drastic devaluation of the rupiah. The effects of the crisis lingered through 1998. In the Philippines growth dropped to virtually zero in 1998. Only Singapore and Taiwan proved relatively insulated from the shock, but both suffered serious hits in passing, the former more so due to its size and geographical location between Malaysia and Indonesia. By

1999, however, analysts saw signs that the economies of Asia were beginning to recover.

CAUSES OF THE CRISIS

Until 1997, Asia attracted almost half of the total capital inflow from developing countries. The economies of Southeast Asia in particular maintained high interest rates attractive to foreign investors looking for a high rate of return. As a result the region's economies received a large inflow of money and experienced a dramatic run-up in asset prices. At the same time, the regional economies of Thailand, Malaysia, Indonesia, Singapore, and South Korea experienced high growth rates, 8-12% GDP, in the late 1980s and early 1990s. This achievement was widely acclaimed by financial institutions including the IMF and World Bank, and was known as part of the "Asian economic miracle".

In 1994, noted economist Paul Krugman published an article attacking the idea of an "Asian economic miracle". He argued that East Asia's economic growth had historically been the result of capital investment, leading to growth in productivity. However, total factor productivity had increased only marginally or not at all. Krugman argued that only growth in total factor productivity, and not capital investment, could lead to long-term prosperity. Krugman's views would be seen by many as prescient after the financial crisis had become full-blown, though he himself stated that he had not predicted the crisis nor foreseen its depth.

The causes of the debacle are many and disputed. Thailand's economy developed into a bubble fueled by "hot money". More and more of the 'hot money' was required as the size of the bubble grew. The same type of situation happened in Malaysia, although Malaysia had better political leadership, and Indonesia, which had the added complication of what was called "crony capitalism". The short-term capital flow was expensive and often highly conditioned for quick profit. Development money went in a largely uncontrolled manner to certain people only, not particularly the best suited or most efficient, but those closest to the centers of power.

At the time of the mid-1990s, Thailand, Indonesia and South Korea had large private current account deficits and the maintenance of fixed exchange rates encouraged external borrowing and led to excessive exposure to foreign exchange risk in both the financial and corporate sectors. In the mid-1990s, two factors began to change their economic environment. As the U.S. economy recovered from a recession in the early 1990s, the U.S. Federal Reserve Bank under Alan Greenspan began to raise U.S. interest rates to head-off inflation. This made the U.S. a more attractive investment destination relative to Southeast Asia, which had attracted hot money flows through high short-term interest rates, and raised the value of the U.S. dollar, to which many Southeast Asian nations' currencies were pegged, thus making their exports less competitive. At the same time, Southeast Asia's export growth slowed dramatically in the spring of 1996, deteriorating their current account position.

Some economists have advanced the impact of China on the real economy as a contributing factor to ASEAN nations' export growth slowdown, though these economists maintain the main cause of the crises was excessive real estate speculation. China had begun to compete effectively with other Asian exporters particularly in the 1990s after the implementation of a number of export-oriented reforms. Most importantly, the Thai and Indonesian currencies were closely tied to the dollar, which was appreciating in the 1990s. Western importers sought cheaper manufacturers and found them, indeed, in China whose currency was depreciated relative to the dollar. Other economists dispute this claim noting that both ASEAN and China experienced simultaneous rapid export growth in the early 1990s.

Many economists believe that the Asian crisis was created not by market psychology or technology, but by policies that distorted incentives within the lender-borrower relationship. The resulting large quantities of credit that became available generated a highly-leveraged economic climate, and pushed up asset prices to an unsustainable level. These asset prices eventually began to collapse, causing individuals and companies to default on debt obligations. The resulting panic among lenders led to a large withdrawal of credit from the crisis countries, causing a credit crunch and further bankruptcies. In addition, as investors attempted to withdraw their money, the exchange market was flooded with the currencies of the crisis countries, putting depreciative pressure on their exchange rates. In order to prevent a collapse of the currency values, these countries' governments were forced to raise domestic interest rates to exceedingly high levels (to help diminish the flight of capital by making lending to that country relatively more attractive to investors) and to intervene in the exchange market, buying up any excess domestic currency at the fixed exchange rate with foreign reserves. Neither of these policy responses could be sustained for long. Very high interest rates, which can be extremely damaging to an economy that is relatively healthy, wreaked further havoc on economies in an already fragile state, while the central banks were hemorrhaging foreign reserves, of which they had finite amounts. When it became clear that the tide of capital fleeing these countries was not to be stopped, the authorities ceased defending their fixed exchange rates and allowed their currencies to float. The resulting depreciated value of those currencies meant that foreign currency-denominated liabilities grew substantially in domestic currency terms, causing more bankruptcies and further deepening the crisis.

Other economists, including Joseph Stiglitz and Jeffrey Sachs, have downplayed the role of the real economy in the crisis compared to the financial markets due to the speed of the crisis. The rapidity with which the crisis happened has prompted Sachs and others to compare it to a classic bank run prompted by a sudden risk shock. Sachs pointed to strict monetary and contractory fiscal policies implemented by the governments on the advice of the IMF in the wake of the crisis, while Frederic Mishkin points to the role of asymmetric information in the financial markets that led to a "herd mentality" among investors that magnified a relatively small risk in the real economy. The crisis had thus attracted interest from behavioural economists interested in market psychology. Another possible cause of the sudden risk shock may also be attributable to the handover of Hong Kong sovereignty on 1 July 1997. During the 1990s, hot money flew into the Southeast

Asia region but investors were often ignorant of the actual fundamentals or risk profiles of the respective economies. The uncertainty regarding the future of Hong Kong led investors to shrink even further away from Asia, exacerbating economic conditions in the area (subsequently leading to the devaluation of the Thai baht on 2 July 1997).

The foreign ministers of the 10 ASEAN countries believed that the well coordinated manipulation of currencies was a deliberate attempt to destabilize the ASEAN economies. Former Malaysian Prime Minister Mahathir Mohammad accused George Soros of ruining Malaysia's economy with "massive currency speculation." (Soros appeared to have had his bets in against the Asian currency devaluations, incurring a loss when the crisis hit.) At the 30th ASEAN Ministerial Meeting held in Subang Jaya, Malaysia, they issued a joint declaration on 25 July 1997 expressing serious concern and called for further intensification of ASEAN's cooperation to safeguard and promote ASEAN's interest in this regard. Coincidentally, on that same day, the central bankers of most of the affected countries were at the EMEAP (Executive Meeting of East Asia Pacific) meeting in Shanghai, and they failed to make the 'New Arrangement to Borrow' operational. A year earlier, the finance ministers of these same countries had attended the 3rd APEC finance ministers meeting in Kyoto, Japan on 17 March 1996, and according to that joint declaration, they had been unable to double the amounts available under the 'General Agreement to Borrow' and the 'Emergency Finance Mechanism'. As such, the crisis could be seen as the failure to adequately build capacity in time to prevent Currency Manipulation. This hypothesis enjoyed little support among economists, however, who argue that no single investor could have had enough impact on the market to successfully manipulate the currencies' values. In addition, the level of organization necessary to coordinate a massive exodus of investors from Southeast Asian currencies in order to manipulate their values rendered this possibility remote.

THE ROLE OF IMF

The scope and the severity of the collapses were such that

outside intervention, considered by many as a new kind of colonialism, and became urgently needed. Since the countries melting down were among not only the richest in their region, but in the world, and since hundreds of billions of dollars were at stake, any response to the crisis had to be cooperative and international. In this case the International Monetary Fund (IMF) came forward. The IMF created a series of bailouts for the most affected economies to enable affected nations to avoid default, tying the packages to reforms that were intended to make the Asian currency restored, banking, and financial systems as much like those of the United States and Europe as possible. In other words, the IMF's support was conditional on a series of drastic economic reforms influenced by neo liberal economic principles called a "structural adjustment package" (SAP). The SAPs called on crisis-struck nations to cut back on government spending to reduce deficits, allow insolvent banks and financial institutions to fail, and aggressively raise interest rates. The reasoning was that these steps would restore confidence in the nations' fiscal solvency, penalize insolvent companies, and protect currency values. Above all, it was stipulated that IMF-funded capital had to be administered rationally in the future, with no favoured parties receiving funds by preference. There were to be adequate government controls set-up to supervise all financial activities, ones that were to be independent, in theory, of private interest. Insolvent institutions had to be closed, and insolvency itself had to be clearly defined. In short, exactly the same kinds of financial institutions found in the United States and Europe had to be created in Asia, as a condition for IMF support. In addition, financial systems had to become "transparent" that is; provide the kind of reliable financial information used in the West to make sound financial decisions.

However, the greatest criticism of the IMF's role in the crisis was targeted towards its response. As country after country fell into crisis, many local businesses and governments that had taken out loans in US dollars, which suddenly became much more expensive relative to the local currency which formed their earned income, found themselves unable to pay their creditors. The dynamics of the situation were closely similar to that of the Latin American debt crisis. The effects of the SAPs were mixed and their impact controversial. Critics, however, noted the contractionary nature of these policies, arguing that in a recession, the traditional Keynesian response was to increase government spending, prop up major companies, and lower interest rates. The reasoning was that by stimulating the economy and staving-off recession, governments could restore confidence while preventing economic loss. They pointed out that the U.S. government had pursued expansionary policies, such as lowering interest rates, increasing government spending, and cutting taxes, when the United States itself entered a recession in 2001.

Although such reforms were, in most cases, long needed, the countries most involved ended up undergoing an almost complete political and financial restructuring. They suffered permanent currency devaluations, massive numbers of bankruptcies, and collapses of whole sectors of once-booming economies, real estate busts, high unemployment, and social unrest. For most of the countries involved, IMF intervention has been roundly criticized. The role of the IMF was so controversial during the crisis that many locals called this financial crisis as the "IMF crisis". To begin with, many commentators in retrospect criticized the IMF for encouraging the developing economies of Asia down the path of "fast track capitalism", meaning liberalization of the financial sector (elimination of restrictions on capital flows); maintenance of high domestic interest rates in order to suck in portfolio investment and bank capital; and pegging of the national currency to the dollar to reassure foreign investors against currency risk. In other words, the IMF itself was the cause of the crisis.

IMF AND HIGH INTEREST RATES

The conventional high-interest-rate economic wisdom is normally employed by monetary authorities to attain the chain objectives of tightened money supply, discouraged currency speculation, stabilized exchange rate, curbed currency depreciation, and ultimately contained inflation. In the Asian meltdown, highest IMF officials rationalized their prescribed high interest rates, as follows:

From then IMF First Deputy Managing Director, Stanley Fischer in a forum funds lecture at UCLA, Los Angeles on March 20, 1998 on the topic IMF and Asian Crisis explain that when the governments of the countries approached the IMF, the reserves of Thailand and Korea were perilously low and the Indonesian Rupiah was excessively depreciated. Thus, the first order of business was to restore confidence in the currency. To achieve this, countries have to make it more attractive to hold domestic currency, which in turn, requires increasing interest rates temporarily, even if higher interest costs complicate the situation of weak banks and corporations.

Unfortunately, IMF's high-interest-rate prescription in the Asian turmoil was quite controversial because it was not the moderate increase in interest rates of usually fraction of one percent, as done in both advanced and developing nations during normal times, but bad-loan provoking high bank lending rates of as much as 60%, as actually implemented during the crisis, especially in the Philippines and Indonesia which had to bear peak non-prime high interest rates of up to 40% and 65%, respectively. The high interest rates were a matter of record in the crisis-hit Asian nations. High interest rates, with had the following objectionable features and fallacies in the past crisis are given as follows:

(1) High Interest Rates were objectionable because these were not a necessary evil. These were merely a product of IMF's failure to prescribe exchange rate hedging on foreign loans of dollar-debt-ridden Asian corporations before the Asian crisis. As prime mover of currency liberalization under globalization, IMF helped in promoting the free flow of advanced nations' massive investment funds to developing Asian countries. The foreign fund inflow fueled the phenomenal growth of affected Asian economies before the crisis. However, as the funds are in effect direct and indirect lending to the developing nations, in the long-run, there is probability that future collections maybe marred by delinquencies and bad

loans, especially if there are economic aberrations. Therefore, as part of IMF's planning and risk management, it should have instituted safety nets to currency liberalization, like prescribing exchange rate hedging on foreign loans obtained by dollar-debt-ridden Asian corporations. Fees to be incurred on exchange rate hedging by the Asian corporations before crisis are definitely less catastrophic than high interest rates to be imposed on third-party borrowers once crisis suddenly strikes. When IMF did nothing and the Asian crisis erupted, naturally, it had to face an onrushing tsunami of exchange losses among dollar-debt ridden Asian companies—which losses would translate to bad loans in the origins of the massive investment funds that flowed into the region. To address the problem, IMF had to prescribe ultra high interest rates aimed at tightening money supply, fighting currency speculation, stabilizing the exchange rate, curbing currency depreciation, and minimizing exchange losses on foreign loans of dollar-debt-ridden Asian corporations—at the sacrifice of Asian borrowers and banks, which had to contend with massive loan defaults and bad loans from unbearable high interest rates.

(2) IMF prescribed high interest rates constituted pointless pursuit of tight monetary policy during the Asian meltdown. One of the most criticized IMF measures was its pointless pursuit of tight monetary policy through the policy tool high interest rates under unsuitable conditions of the Asian crisis. Even in the midst of raging economic crisis, it did not follow that tight monetary policy had to be instituted through usual tight-money measures. Other economic stimuli or events could also provoke tight-money conditions even without high interest rates. In the Asian financial crisis, the stimulating events that automatically produced tight-money conditions, which in turn rendered IMF's tight monetary policy a costly but superfluous exercise, were as follows:

(a) Impending or already prevailing drained liquidity in the economy, brought about by massive capital flight, including cut off of banking credits, which ballooned to $ 203 billion in the five crisis-hit Asian countries—Thailand, South Korea, Malaysia, Indonesia, and the Philippines as IMF could not fill with enough bailout funds the void left by the staggering capital flight, the drained liquidity was real, hence the United States had to earmark $ 18 billion quota contribution to IMF, while Japan had to supplement with $ 30 billion Miyazawa fund the limited IMF bailout funds, to help resuscitate the dehydrated Asian economies.

(b) Tight cash position of banks due to the resulting "maturities mismatch" in the banking system, or the sudden withdrawal of scared short-term foreign funds that fled to safe investment havens upon the outbreak of crisis, when these volatile funds had been lent out on long-term or renewable basis by the banks.

(c) Lack of inflationary build-up of money supply in the economy owing to negligible flow of money from banks to borrowers then to the spending public, as a result of difficulties and uncertainties in the crisis. Banks suffering from tight cash position as an offshoot of massive capital flight generally cancelled unused credit lines of clients and temporarily halted their lending to prospective borrowers. Both investors and banks were simply on a wait-and-see stance while the crisis raged.

(3) Ultra High Interest Rates Provoked Massive Loan Defaults and Bad Loans in the Asian Turbulence. The following is the situation of bad loans in the different countries:

- *Indonesia*: problem loans-75% of total loans as of

1999; required bank recapitalization-$ 90 billion.

- *Thailand*: problem loans-42% of total as of November 1999; bad loans-$ 63 billion.
- *South Korea*: problem loans-30% of total by end 1999; required bank recapitalization-$ 50 billion.
- *Malaysia*: problem loans-30% of total by early 2000; required bank recapitalization-$ 15 billion.
- *Philippines*: problem loans-31% as of 2001 and 36% as of 2002; bad loans-$ 9 billion as of 2001 and $ 11 billion as of 2002.

Consequently, in 1998 IMF had to arrange the following bailout funds for crisis-hit Asian countries that sought its financial assistance. They are South Korea [$ 58 billion]; Indonesia [$ 42 billion]; and Thailand [$ 17 billion].

(4) IMF's high-interest-rate prescription was a back-breaking subsidy scheme and unjust taxation of borrowers in the Crisis. Through its prescribed high interest rates as solution to national economic crisis, IMF compelled a relatively few borrowers to shoulder the responsibility of the entire nation. As applied to the Philippines, this meant an estimated three million borrowers, or roughly 4% of total population, financing exclusively a heavy cost of solving the economic crisis for the benefit of 76 million Philippines, with freeloading non-borrowers similarly benefiting from the solution but not sharing in its cost. Among other things, the high-interest-rate subsidy scheme equates to unjust taxation of borrowers. As the increases in interest rates were no longer cost of using borrowed money but cost of pursuing the governmental function of addressing the financial crisis and ultimately containing inflation, it is a public expenditure for the common good of the people. Therefore, it should be financed by taxes or other funds emanating from the whole benefiting nation.

(5) IMF-prescribed 60% ultra high interest rate in acute economic crisis is questionable because it is anchored

on the illogical premise that the need for high interest rates is directly-not inversely-proportional to the severity of economic crisis. IMF's 60% ultra high-interest-rate prescription implies that the need for high interest rates is directly proportional to the severity of economic crisis, that is, the more severe the crisis, the more need for higher interest rates in tightening money supply, maintaining investor confidence, stopping capital flight, and so on as in the case of the 65% ultra high interest rate in Indonesia when it went through combined political-economic convulsion in 1998.

In reality, the reverse appears true that the need for high interest rates is inversely proportional to the intensity of crisis. In a situation of ultra economic crisis, especially if attended to by political turbulence or threat of civil war, other economic factors such as mass capital flight and more pronounced slump in borrowing and lending come into greater play and diminish much more the role of high interest rates as tight-money policy tool, through automatically constricting severely the existing money supply and thereby rendering superfluous the tight-money-measure high interest rates.

(6) IMF's high-interest-rate prescription as antidote to currency speculation is unnecessary because there is an obvious, practical, and less disastrous alternative to it—running directly after currency speculators, as already tested and successfully done in the Philippines. With currency speculation that undermines the exchange rate as main problem during currency turmoil, the solution was not ultra high interest rates but running all-out after speculators as successfully done in the Philippines in August 2001.

THAILAND AND THE CRISIS

From 1985 to 1996, Thailand's economy grew at an average of over 9% per year, the highest economic growth rate of any country at that time. In 1996, an American hedge fund sold US $ 400 million of the Thai currency. On 14 May and 15 May 1997, the Thai baht was hit by massive speculative attacks. On 30 June 1997, Prime Minister Chavalit Yongchaiyudh said that he would not devalue the baht. This was the spark that ignited the Asian financial crisis as the Thai government failed to defend the baht, which was pegged to the U.S. dollar, against international speculators. Thailand's booming economy came to a halt amid massive layoffs in finance, real estate, and construction that resulted in huge numbers of workers returning to their villages in the countryside and 6,00,000 foreign workers being sent back to their home countries. The baht devalued swiftly and lost more than half of its value. The baht reached its lowest point of 56 units to the US dollar in January 1998. The Thai stock market dropped 75%.

The Thai government was eventually forced to float the Baht on 2 July 1997. On 11 August 1997, the IMF unveiled a rescue package for Thailand with more than $ 17 billion, subject to conditions such as passing laws relating to bankruptcy (reorganizing and restructuring) procedures and establishing strong regulation frameworks for banks and other financial institutions. The IMF approved on 20 August, 1997, another bailout package of $ 3.9 billion.

Thai opposition parties claimed that former Prime Minister Thaksin Shinawatra had profited from the devaluation, it is now being investigated by the court of justice. However, there are statement from the witnesses stated that Thaksin Shinawatra was in the meeting room during the decision-making process which he shouldn't be allowed to appear.

By 2001, Thailand's economy had recovered. The increasing tax revenues allowed the country to balance its budget and repay its debts to the IMF in 2003, four years ahead of schedule. The Thai baht continued to appreciate to 34 Baht to the Dollar in July 2008.

INDONESIA AND THE CRISIS

In June 1997, Indonesia seemed far from crisis. Unlike

Thailand, Indonesia had low inflation, a trade surplus of more than $ 900 million, huge foreign exchange reserves of more than $ 20 billion, and a good banking sector. But a large number of Indonesian corporations had been borrowing in U.S. dollars. During the preceding years, as the rupiah had strengthened respective to the dollar, this practice had worked well for these corporations; their effective levels of debt and financing costs had decreased as the local currency's value rose.

In July 1997, when Thailand floated the baht, Indonesia's monetary authorities widened the rupiah trading band from 8% to 12%. The rupiah suddenly came under severe attack in August. On 14 August 1997, the managed floating exchange regime was replaced by a free-floating exchange rate arrangement. The rupiah dropped further. The IMF came forward with a rescue package of $ 23 billion, but the rupiah was sinking further amid fears over corporate debts, massive selling of rupiah, and strong demand for dollars. The rupiah and the Jakarta Stock Exchange touched a historic low in September, 1997. Moody's eventually downgraded Indonesia's long-term debt to 'junk bond'.

Although the rupiah crisis began in July and August 1997, it intensified in November when the effects of that summer devaluation showed up on corporate balance sheets. Companies that had borrowed in dollars had to face the higher costs imposed upon them by the rupiah's decline, and many reacted by buying dollars through selling rupiah, undermining the value of the latter further. The inflation of the rupiah and the resulting steep hikes in the prices of food staples led to rioting throughout the country in which more than 500 people died in Jakarta alone. In February 1998, President Suharto sacked the governor of Bank Indonesia, but this had proved insufficient. Suharto was forced to resign in mid-1998 and B.J. Habibie became President. Before the crisis, the exchange rate between the rupiah and the dollar was roughly 2000 rupiah to 1 USD. The rate had plunged to over 18000 rupiah to 1 USD at various points during the crisis. Indonesia lost 13.5% of its GDP that year.

SOUTH KOREA AND THE CRISIS

Macroeconomic fundamentals in South Korea were good but the banking sector was burdened with non-performing loans as its large corporations were funding aggressive expansions. During that time, there was a haste to build great conglomerates to compete on the world stage. Many businesses ultimately failed to ensure returns and profitability. The Korean conglomerates, more or less completely controlled by the government, simply absorbed more and more capital investment. Eventually, excess debt led to major failures and takeovers. For example, in July 1997, South Korea's third-largest car maker, Kia Motors, asked for emergency loans. In the wake of the Asian market downturn, Moody's lowered the credit rating of South Korea from A1 to A3, on 28 November 1997, and downgraded again to B2 on 11 December. That contributed to a further decline in Korean shares since stock markets were already bearish in November. The Seoul stock exchange fell by 4% on 7 November 1997. On 8 November, it plunged by 7%, its biggest one-day drop to that date. And on 24 November, stocks fell a further 7.2% on fears that the IMF would demand tough reforms. In 1998, Hyundai Motor took over Kia Motors. Samsung Motors' $ 5 billion dollar venture was dissolved due to the crisis, and eventually Daewoo Motors was sold to the American company General Motors (GM).

The South Korean currency won, meanwhile, weakened to more than 1,700 per dollar from around 800. Despite an initial sharp economic slowdown and numerous corporate bankruptcies, Korea has managed to triple its per capita GDP in dollar terms since 1997. Indeed, it resumed its role as the world's fastest-growing economy—since 1960, per capita GDP has grown from $ 80 in nominal terms to more than $ 21,000 as of 2007. However, like the chaebol (The Korean word means "business family" or "monopoly" and is often used the way "conglomerate" is used in English), South Korea's government did not escape unscathed. Its national debt-to-GDP ratio became more than doubled (app. 13% to 30%) as a result of the crisis. In Korea, the crisis is also commonly referred to as the *IMF crisis*.

PHILIPPINES AND THE CRISIS

The Philippine central bank raised interest rates by 1.75 percentage points in May 1997 and again by 2 points on 19 June, 1997. Thailand triggered the crisis on 2 July and on 3 July; the Philippine Central Bank was forced to intervene heavily to defend the peso, raising the overnight rate from 15% to 32% right upon the onset of the Asian crisis in mid-July 1997. The peso fell significantly, from 26 pesos per dollar at the start of the crisis, to 38 pesos as of mid-1999, and to 54 pesos as of first half August 2001.

The Philippine economy recovered from a contraction of 0.6% in GDP during the worst part of the crisis to GDP growth of some 3% by 2001, despite scandals of the administration of Joseph Estrada in 2001, most notably the "jueteng" scandal, causing the PSE Composite Index, the main index of the Philippine Stock Exchange, to fall to some 1000 points from a high of some 3000 points in 1997. The peso fell even further, trading at levels of about 55 pesos to the US dollar. Later that year, Estrada was on the verge of impeachment but his allies in the senate voted against the proceedings to continue further. This led to popular protests culminating in the "EDSA II Revolution", which finally forced his resignation and elevated Gloria Macapagal-Arroyo to the presidency. Arroyo managed to lessen the crisis in the country, which led to the recovery of the Philippine peso to about 50 pesos by the year's end and traded at around 41 pesos to a dollar by end 2007. The stock market also reached an all time high in 2007 and the economy is growing by at least more than 7 percent, it's highest in nearly 2 decades.

HONG KONG AND THE CRISIS

Although the two events were unrelated, the collapse of the Thai baht on 2 July 1997 came only 24 hours after the United Kingdom handed over sovereignty of Hong Kong to the People's Republic of China. In October 1997, the Hong Kong dollar, which had been pegged at 7.8 to the U.S. dollar since 1983, came under speculative pressure because Hong Kong's inflation rate had been significantly higher than the

U.S.'s for years. Monetary authorities spent more than US$ 1 billion to defend the local currency. Since Hong Kong had more than US$ 80 billion in foreign reserves, which is equivalent to 700% of its M1 money supply and 45% of its M3 money supply, the Hong Kong Monetary Authority (effectively the city's central bank) managed to maintain the peg.

Stock markets became more and more volatile; between 20 October and 23 October the Hang Seng Index dropped 23%. The Hong Kong Monetary Authority [HKMA] then promised to protect the currency. On 15 August 1998, it raised overnight interest rates from 8% to 23% and at one point to 500%. The HKMA had recognized that speculators were taking advantage of the city's unique currency-board system, in which overnight rates automatically increase in proportion to large net sales of the local currency. The rate hike, however, increased downward pressure on the stock market, allowing speculators to profit by short selling shares. The HKMA started buying component shares of the Hang Seng Index in mid-August. The HKMA and Donald Tsang, then the Financial Secretary, declared war on speculators. The Government ended up buying approximately HK$ 120 billion (US $ 15 billion) worth of shares in various companies, and became the largest shareholder of some of those companies (e.g. the government owned 10% of HSBC) at the end of August, when hostilities ended with the closing of the August Hang Seng Index futures contract. The Government started selling those shares in 2001, making a profit of about HK$ 30 billion (US$ 4 billion).

MALAYSIA AND THE CRISIS

Before the crisis, Malaysia had a large current account deficit of 5% of its GDP. At that time, Malaysia was a popular investment destination, and this was reflected in Kuala Lumpur Stock Exchange [KLSE] activity which was regularly the most active stock exchange in the world (with turnover exceeding even markets with far higher capitalization like the NYSE). Expectations at the time were that the growth rate would continue, propelling Malaysia to developed status by 2020, a government policy articulated in Wawasan 2020. At the start of 1997, the KLSE Composite index was above 1,200, the ringgit, the Malaysian currency was trading above 2.50 to the dollar, and the overnight rate was below 7%.

In July 1997, within days of the Thai baht devaluation, the Malaysian ringgit was "attacked" by speculators. The overnight rate jumped from under 8% to over 40%. This led to rating downgrades and a general sell-off on the stock and currency markets. By end of 1997, ratings had fallen many notches from investment grade to junk, the KLSE had lost more than 50% from above 1,200 to lower than 600, and the ringgit had lost 50% of its value, falling from above 2.50 to under 3.80 to the dollar.

In 1998, the output of the real economy declined plunging the country into its first recession for many years. The construction sector contracted 23.5%, manufacturing shrunk 9% and the agriculture sector 5.9%. Overall, the country's gross domestic product plunged 6.2% in 1998. During that year, the ringgit plunged below 4.7 and the KLSE fell below 270 points. In September that year, various defensive measures were announced in order to overcome the crisis. The principal measures taken were to move the ringgit from a free float to a fixed exchange rate regime. Bank Negara fixed the ringgit at 3.8 to the dollar. Capital controls were imposed while aid offered from the IMF was refused. Various task force agencies were formed. The Corporate Debt Restructuring Committee dealt with corporate loans Danaharta discounted and bought bad loans from banks to facilitate orderly asset realization.

Growth then settled at a slower but more sustainable pace. The massive current account deficit became a fairly substantial surplus. Banks were better capitalized and Non Performing Loans [NPLs] were realized in an orderly way. Small banks were bought out by strong ones. A large number of Prime Lending Corporations [PLCs] were unable to regulate their financial affairs and were delisted. Compared to the 1997 current account, by 2005, Malaysia was estimated to have a US$ 14.06 billion surplus. Asset values however, have not returned to their pre-crisis highs. In 2005 the last of the crisis measures were removed as the ringgit was taken-off the fixed exchange system. But unlike the pre-crisis days, it did not appear to be a free float, but a managed float, like the Singapore dollar.

SINGAPORE AND THE CRISIS

As the financial crisis spread, the economy of Singapore dipped into a short recession. The relatively short duration and milder effect on its economy was credited to the active management by the government. For example, the Monetary Authority of Singapore allowed for a gradual 20% depreciation of the Singapore dollar to cushion and guide the economy to a soft landing. The timing of government programs such as the Interim Upgrading Program and other construction related projects were brought forward. Instead of allowing the labor markets to work, the National Wage Council pre-emptively agreed to Central Provident Fund cuts to lower labor costs, with limited impact on disposable income and local demand. Unlike in Hong Kong, no attempt was made to directly intervene in the capital markets and the Straits Times Index was allowed to drop 60%. In less than a year, the Singaporean economy fully recovered and continued on its growth trajectory.

CHINA AND THE CRISIS

The Chinese currency, the Renminbi (RMB), had been pegged to the US dollar at a ratio of 8.3 RMB to the dollar, in 1994. Having largely kept itself above the fray throughout 1997-1998 there was heavy speculation in the Western press that China would soon be forced to devalue its currency to protect the competitiveness of its exports *vis-à-vis* those of the ASEAN nations, whose exports became cheaper relative to China's. However, the RMB's non-convertibility protected its value from currency speculators, and the decision was made to maintain the peg of the currency, thereby improving the country's standing within Asia. The currency peg was partly scrapped in July 2005 rising 2.3% against the dollar, reflecting pressure from the United States.

Unlike investments of many of the Southeast Asian nations, almost all of China's foreign investment took the form of factories on the ground rather than securities, which insulated the country from rapid capital flight. China was relatively unaffected by the crisis compared to Southeast Asia and South Korea. GDP growth slowed sharply in 1998 and 1999, calling attention to structural problems within its economy. In particular, the Asian financial crisis convinced the Chinese government of the need to resolve the issues of its enormous financial weaknesses, such as having too many non-performing loans within its primitive and inefficient banking system, and relying heavily on trade with the United States.

US AND JAPAN AND CRISIS

The "Asian flu" had also put pressure on the United States and Japan. Their markets did not collapse, but they were severely hit. On 27 October 1997, the Dow Jones Industrial Average [DJIA] plunged 554 points or 7.2%, amid ongoing worries about the Asian economies. The New York Stock Exchange briefly suspended trading. The crisis led to a drop in consumer and spending confidence. Japan was affected because its economy is prominent in the region. Asian countries usually run a trade deficit with Japan because the latter's economy was more than twice the size of the rest of Asia together; about 40% of Japan's exports go to Asia. The Japanese yen fell to 147 as mass selling began, but Japan was the world's largest holder of currency reserves at the time, so it was easily defended, and quickly bounced back. GDP real growth rate slowed dramatically in 1997, from 5% to 1.6% and even sank into recession in 1998, due to intense competition from cheapened rivals. The Asian financial crisis also led to more bankruptcies in Japan. In addition, with South Korea's devalued currency, and China's steady gains, many companies complained outright that they could not compete.

Another longer-term result was the changing relationship between the U.S. and Japan, with the U.S. no longer openly supporting the highly artificial trade environment and exchange rates that governed economic relations between the two countries for almost five decades after World War II.

CONSEQUENCES OF THE CRISIS

Asia

The crisis had significant macro-level effects, including

TABLE 8.1

Change in the Currency Value and GNP of Major Asian Countries

Currency	*Exchange rate (per US $ 1)*		*Change*	*Country*	*GNP (US $ 1 billion)*		*Change*
	June 1997	*July 1998*			*June 1997*	*July 1998*	
(1)	*(2)*	*(3)*	*(4)*	*(5)*	*(6)*	*(7)*	*(8)*
Thai baht	24.5	41	-40.20%	Thailand	170	102	-40.00%
Indonesian rupiah	2,380	14,150	-83.20%	Indonesia	205	34	-83.40%
Philippine peso	26.3	42	-37.40%	Philippines	75	47	-37.30%
Malaysian ringgit	2.5	4.1	-39.00%	Malaysia	90	55	-38.90%
South Korean won	850	1,290	-34.10%	South Korea	430	283	-34.20%

sharp reductions in values of currencies, stock markets, and other asset prices of several Asian countries. The nominal US dollar GDP of ASEAN fell by US$ 9.2 billion in 1997 and $ 218.2 billion (31.7%) in 1998. In Korea, the $ 170.9 billion fall in 1998 was equal to 33.1% of the 1997 GDP. Many businesses collapsed, and as a consequence, millions of people fell below the poverty line in 1997-98. Indonesia, South Korea and Thailand were the countries most affected by the crisis. The following table shows the change in the currency value and GNP of the different Asian countries between 1997 to 1998.

The economic crisis also led to a political upheaval, most notably culminating in the resignations of President Suharto in Indonesia and Prime Minister General Chavalit Yongchaiyudh in Thailand. There was a general rise in anti-Western sentiment, with George Soros and the IMF in particular singled out as targets of criticisms. Heavy U.S. investment in Thailand ended, replaced by mostly European investment, though Japanese investment was sustained. Islamic and other separatist movements intensified in Southeast Asia as central authorities weakened.

More long-term consequences included reversal of the relative gains made in the boom years just preceding the crisis. Nominal US dollar GDP per capital fell 42.3% in Indonesia in 1997, 21.2% in Thailand, 19% in Malaysia, 18.5% in Korea and 12.5% in the Philippines. The CIA World Fact book reported that the per capita income (measured by purchasing power parity) in Thailand declined from $ 8,800 to $ 8,300 between 1997 and 2005; in Indonesia it declined from $ 4,600 to $ 3,700; in Malaysia it declined from $ 11,100 to $ 10,400. Over the same period, world per capita income rose from $ 6,500 to $ 9,300. Indeed, the CIA's analysis asserted that the economy of Indonesia was still smaller in 2005 than it had been in 1997, suggesting an impact on that country similar to that of the Great Depression. Within East Asia, the bulk of investment and a significant amount of economic weight shifted from Japan and ASEAN to *China and India*.

Outside Asia

After the Asian crisis, international investors were reluctant to lend to developing countries, leading to economic slowdowns in developing countries in many parts of the world. The powerful negative shock also sharply reduced the price of oil, which reached a low of $ 8 per barrel towards the end of 1998, causing a financial pinch in OPEC nations and other oil exporters. This reduction in oil revenue contributed to the 1998 Russian financial crisis, which in turn caused Long-Term Capital Management in the United States to collapse after losing $ 4.6 billion in 4 months. A wider collapse in the financial markets was avoided when Alan Greenspan and the Federal Reserve Bank of New York organized a $ 3.625 billion bail-out. Major emerging economies Brazil and Argentina also fell into crisis in the late 1990s.

CONCLUSION

The crisis has been intensively analyzed by economists for its breadth, speed, and dynamism; it affected dozens of countries, had a direct impact on the livelihood of millions, happened within the course of a mere few months, and at each stage of the crisis leading economists, in particular the international institutions, seemed a step behind. Perhaps more interesting to economists was the speed with which it ended, leaving most of the developed economies unharmed. A number of critiques have been leveled against the conduct of the IMF in the crisis. Politically there were some benefits. In several countries, particularly South Korea and Indonesia, there was renewed push for improved corporate governance. Rampaging inflation weakened the authority of the Suharto regime and led to its toppling in 1998, as well as accelerating East Timor's independence. The crisis could be seen as the failure to adequately build capacity in time to prevent Currency Manipulation, as it is seen that the currency speculation was one of the major cause of the crisis. The crisis also teach the lesson that how a crisis situation can be overcome by the government wisely and active role and without any foreign help as the aid from the IMF was refused by Malaysia and because of the active management of the government of Singapore the crisis was ended there.

Russian Financial Crisis

The *Russian financial crisis* is also called as the Rubble Crisis. It hit Russia on 17 August 1998. It was triggered by the Asian financial crisis, which started in July 1997. Because of the Asian Financial Crisis there was the ensuing decline in world commodity prices especially of crude oil. Those countries that are heavily dependent on the export of raw materials were among those most severely hit. Russian is basically the exporter of petroleum, natural gas, metals, and timber products. These accounted for more than 80% of Russian exports, leaving the country vulnerable to swings in world prices. Oil was also a major source of government tax revenue.

Overview of the Chapter

The present chapter highlights the Russian Financial Crisis which was resulted out of Asian Financial Crisis. The chapter highlights the following important headings:

- Causes of the Crisis
- Effect of the Crisis
- Political Fallout of the Crisis
- Recovery from the Crisis
- Effect on Other Countries
- Conclusion

CAUSES OF THE CRISIS

Prior to the culmination of the economic crisis, the government-issued GKO bonds policy. It had been described as similar to a pyramid scheme or Ponzi scheme as the interest on matured obligations being paid-off using the proceeds of newly issued obligations.

Declining productivity, an artificially high fixed exchange rate between the ruble and foreign currencies to avoid public turmoil, and a chronic fiscal deficit were the background to the meltdown. The economic cost of the first war in Chechnya that is estimated at $ 5.5 billion (not including the rebuilding of the ruined Chechen economy) was also a cause of the crisis. In the first half of 1997, the Russian economy showed some signs of improvement. However, soon after this, the problems began to gradually intensify. Two external shocks, the Asian financial crisis that had begun in 1997 and the following declines in demand for (and thus price of) crude oil and non-ferrous metals, also impacted Russian foreign exchange reserves. A political crisis came to a head in March when Russian president Boris Yeltsin suddenly dismissed Prime Minister Viktor Chernomyrdin and his entire cabinet on March 23, 1997. Yeltsin named Energy Minister Sergei Kiriyenko, aged 35, as acting prime minister. On May 29, 1997, Yeltsin appointed Boris Fyodorov, Head of the State Tax Service. The growth of internal loans could only be provided at the expense of the inflow of foreign speculative capital, which was attracted by very high interest rates. In an effort to prop up the currency and stem the flight of capital, in June Kiriyenko hiked GKO interest rates to 150%. The situation was worsened by irregular internal debt payments. Despite government efforts the debts and the wages continued to grow, especially in the remote regions. By the end of 1997, the situation with the tax receipts was very tense, and it had a negative effect on the financing of the major budget items (pensions, communal utilities, transportation, etc.). A $ 22.6 billion International Monetary Fund and World Bank financial package was approved on July 13, 1997 to support reforms and stabilize the Russian market by swapping out an enormous volume of the quickly maturing GKO short-term bills into long-term Eurobonds. This had started to be implemented with some success by July 24, 1997 yet the Russian government decided to keep the exchange rate of the ruble within a narrow band, although many economists, including Andrei Illarionov and George Soros, urged the government to abandon its support to the ruble. On May 12, 1998 Coal miners went on strike over unpaid wages, blocking the Trans-Siberian Railway. By August 1, 1998 there were approximately $ 12.5 billion in unpaid wages account owed to Russian workers. On August 14, 1998 the exchange rate of the Russian ruble to the US dollar was still 6.29. Despite the bailout, July monthly interest payments on Russia's debt rose to a figure 40 percent greater than its monthly tax collections. Additionally, on July 15, 1998 the State Duma dominated by left-wing parties refused to adopt most of government anti-crisis plan so that the government was forced to rely on presidential decrees. On July 29, 1998 Yeltsin interrupted his vacation in Valdai Lake region and flew to Moscow, prompting fears of a Cabinet reshuffle, but he only replaced Federal Security Service Chief Nikolai Kovalyov with Vladimir Putin.

At the time, Russia employed a "floating peg" policy toward the ruble, meaning that the Central Bank at any given time committed that the ruble-to-dollar (or RUR/USD) exchange rate would stay within a particular range. If the ruble threatened to devalue outside of that range (or "band"), the Central Bank would intervene by spending foreign reserves to buy rubles. For instance, during approximately the one year prior to the Crisis, the Central Bank committed to maintain a band of 5.3 to 7.1 RUR/USD meaning that it would buy rubles if the market exchange rate threatened to exceed 7.1 rubles per dollar.

The manifest inability of the Russian government to implement a coherent set of economic reforms led to severe erosion in investor confidence and a chain-reaction that can be likened to a run on the Central Bank. Investors fled the market by selling rubles and Russian assets (such as securities), which also put downward pressure on the ruble. This forced the Central Bank to spend its foreign reserves to defend the ruble, which in turn further eroded investor confidence and undermined the ruble. It is estimated that between October 1, 1997 and August 17, 1998, the Central Bank expended approximately $ 27 billion of its U.S. dollar reserves to maintain the floating peg.

It was later revealed that about $ 5 billion of the international loans provided by the World Bank and International Monetary Fund were stolen upon the funds' arrival in Russia on the eve of the meltdown.

On August 13, 1998, the Russian stock, bond, and currency markets collapsed as a result of investor fears that the government would devalue the ruble, default on domestic debt, or both. Annual yields on ruble denominated bonds were more than 200 percent. The stock market had to be closed for 35 minutes as prices plummeted. When the market closed, it was down 65 percent with a small number of shares actually traded. From January to August the stock market had lost more than 75 percent of its value, 39 percent in the month of May alone.

EFFECT OF THE CRISIS

On August 17, 1998, the Russian government and the Central Bank of Russia issued a "Joint Statement" announcing, in substance, that: (i) the ruble/dollar trading band would be widened from 5.3-7.1 RUR/USD to 6.0-9.5 RUR/USD; (ii) Russia's ruble-denominated debt would be restructured in a manner to be announced at a later date; and, to prevent mass Russian bank default, (iii) a temporary 90-day moratorium would be imposed on the payment of some bank obligations, including certain debts and forward currency contracts. At the same time, in addition to widening the currency band, the authorities also announced that they intended to allow the RUR/USD rate to move more freely within the wider band.

At the time, the Moscow Inter bank Currency Exchange (or "MICEX") set a daily "official" exchange rate through a series of iterative auctions based on written bids submitted by buyers and sellers. When the buy and sell prices matched this "fixed" or "settled" the official MICEX exchange rate, which would then be published by Reuters. The MICEX rate was (and is) commonly used by banks and currency dealers worldwide as the reference exchange rate for transactions involving the Russian ruble and foreign currencies.

From August 17 to August 25, the ruble steadily depreciated on the MICEX, moving from 6.43 to 7.86 RUR/ USD. On August 26, the Central Bank terminated ruble-dollar trading on the MICEX, and the MICEX did not fix a ruble-dollar rate that day.

On September 2, 1998 the Central Bank of the Russian Federation decided to abandon the "floating peg" policy and float the ruble freely. By September 21, 1998 the exchange rate had reached 21 rubles to the US dollar—meaning it had, stupendously, lost two thirds of its value of less than a month earlier.

On September 28, 1998 Boris Fyodorov was fired from the position of the Head of the State Tax Service.

The moratorium imposed by the Joint Statement expired on November 15, 1998, and the Russian government and Central Bank did not renew it.

Russian inflation in 1998 reached 84 percent and welfare costs grew considerably. Many banks, including Inkombank, Oneximbank and Tokobank, were closed down as a result of the crisis. The salaries of miners alone were to consume $ 919 million, more than 1 percent of the federal budget. By August of that year, the government had paid $ 4 billion to settle miners' strikes. Prices for almost all Russian food items have gone up by almost 100%, while imports have quadrupled in price. Many citizens were stocking up for bad times and throughout the country shop shelves were being emptied, leaving a shortage of even the most basic items, such as vegetable oil, sugar or washing powder. The crisis has reduced demand for food and lowered food consumption, because substantial depreciation of the ruble significantly raises domestic prices for food stuffs. The crisis also increased social tension; The middle class that was already forming by that time, and had some hope for stability, ceased to exist as millions of people lost their bank savings. On October 7 that year, demonstrations were held in many cities: around 100,000 took to the streets in Moscow, In Vladivostok 4,000, in Krasnoyarsk 3,000 and in Yekaterinburg 6,000. Defense Minister Igor Sergeyev cancelled his scheduled visit to Greece in the first week of October, 1998 in order to be at hand should matters get out of control. Similarly select military units were placed in a state of readiness. On 20 October, President Boris Yel'tsin also signed a presidential decree barring "mass protests" in Moscow between the hours of 10 p.m. and 7 a.m. and limiting them to a maximum of five days.

As the crisis deepened, regional governors had been introducing emergency measures: In Krasnoyarsk Krai in Siberia, Governor Aleksandr Lebed, had signed a resolution to hold down prices "using administrative methods", a television report said. The authorities in the far eastern city of Vladivostok had banned deliveries of food to areas beyond the port city, and there had been talks of introducing rationing there. In Russia's Kaliningrad enclave on the Baltic, the governor announced a suspension of tax payments to the federal authorities.

The regional budgets also suffered from the 1998 crisis. The spending of the regions declined from 18.2% of the GDP in 1997 to 14.8% of the GDP. Spending on the economy (by 1.5% of the GDP) and social expenditures (by 1.6% of the GDP) were especially heavily reduced. The expenditures continued to decline in the following period. They dropped another 1% of the GDP in 1999 to 13.8% of the GDP, and to 10.8% of the GDP in the first quarter of 2000. One of the main factors in the reduction was the decline in subsidies for housing and municipal services, from 3.5% to 2.7% of the GDP.

POLITICAL FALLOUT OF THE CRISIS

The financial collapse resulted in a political crisis as Yeltsin, with his domestic support evaporating, had to contend with an emboldened opposition in the parliament. A week later, on August 23, 1998 Yeltsin fired Kiriyenko and declared his intention of returning Chernomyrdin to office as the country slipped deeper into economic turmoil. Powerful business interests, fearing another round of reforms that might cause leading concerns to fail, welcomed Kiriyenko's fall, as did the Communists.

Yeltsin, who began to lose his hold on power as his health deteriorated, wanted Chernomyrdin back; in a televised address to the nation, Yeltsin said that "heavyweights" such as Chernomyrdin, who was ousted as prime minister in March

1998 for failing to vigorously promote economic reforms, were needed to stem the nation's financial collapse. Yeltsin also suggested that Chernomyrdin would be named his successor as president when Yeltsin's term expires in 2000. But the legislature refused to give its approval. After the Duma rejected Chernomyrdin's candidacy twice, Yeltsin, his power clearly on the wane, backed down. Instead, he nominated Foreign Minister Yevgeny Primakov, who on September 11, 1998 was overwhelmingly approved by the Duma.

Primakov's appointment restored political stability, because he was seen as a compromise candidate able to heal the rifts between Russia's quarreling interest groups. There was popular enthusiasm for Primakov as well. Primakov promised to make the payment of wage and pension arrears his government's first priority, and invited members of the leading parliamentary factions into his Cabinet. Communists and the Federation of Independent Trade Unions of Russia staged a nationwide strike on October 7 and called on President Yeltsin to resign. On October 9, Russia, which was also suffering from a bad harvest, appealed for international humanitarian aid, including food.

RECOVERY FROM THE CRISIS

Russia bounced back from the August 1998 financial crisis with surprising speed. Much of the reason for the recovery is that world oil prices rapidly rose during 1999–2000 (just as falling energy prices on the world market helped to deepen Russia's financial troubles), so that Russia ran a large trade surplus in 1999 and 2000. Another reason is that domestic industries, such as food processing, had benefited from the devaluation, which caused a steep increase in the prices of imported goods. Also, since Russia's economy was operating to such a large extent on barter and other non-monetary instruments of exchange, the financial collapse had far less of an impact on many producers than it would had the economy been dependent on a banking system. Finally, the economy has been helped by an infusion of cash; as enterprises were able to pay-off arrears in back wages and taxes, it in turn allowed consumer demand for the goods and services of Russian industry to rise. For the first time in many years, unemployment in 2000 fell as enterprises added workers. Since the 1998 crisis, the Russian government has managed to keep social and political pressures under control, and this has played a vital role in bringing about the current recovery.

EFFECT ON OTHER COUNTRIES

Baltic States

The Russian Rubble crisis affected Baltic countries more than that was expected. It is because of the Rubble Crisis countries like Estonia, Latvia and Lithuania sank into recession. The figures for 1999 showed a heavy decline in Baltic's exports to Russia and a significant decline in the growth rates of these economies. Food and beverage as well as processing industries as a whole have suffered the most.

Belarus

Overall, economic activity slowed down substantially in the immediate aftermath of the Russian crisis, with output growth falling from about 8.5 percent in 1998 to 3.4 percent in 1999. Both exports and imports contracted substantially, resulting in a drop in the current account deficit from 6.1 percent of GDP in 1998 to 2.2 percent of GDP in 1999. Externally, exports to Russia, which accounted for more than 60 percent of total exports, fell during the second half of 1998 by 10 percent. Demand for Belarusian products was weak through 1999, showing signs of recovery only during the final quarter, with the revival of economic activity in Russia. Also, in the first quarter of 1999 as compared with 1998, except for investments, all the budget expenditures were smaller. The biggest cuts were done in national security (1.9 percent of GDP compared with 2.5 percent of GDP in the first quarter of 1998) and social policy (1.5 and 2.4 percent of GDP, respectively), where the expenditures were lowered almost by one third.

Kazakhstan

The Russian crisis was a hard hitting blow to the Kazakh economy. Kazakhstan lost its price competitiveness and its exports were in shambles. On the other hand, cheap Russian goods were flowing into the economy that was killing the domestic industries. There was huge downward pressure on the Tenge. Their balance of payments had worsened. However the NBK was still holding on to the Tenge. In fact, they had spent close to a billion dollars to maintain the level of Tenge. Their foreign exchange reserves halved.

Moldova

Moldova received an IMF special mission advising the government on how to cope with the effects of the Russian crisis. Russia bought at that time 85% of Moldova's wine and brandy and most of its canned goods and tobacco. After the Rubble crashed, most Russian importers put deals with Moldova on hold. Moldovan president Petru Lucinschi was quoted as saying that the Russian crisis had cost Moldova as much as five per cent of its GDP. The country's parliament was discussing a programme aimed at reducing imports and searching for new markets outside Russia.

Ukraine

The crisis cost a lot for Ukraine. The Hryvnia devaluated by 60%, domestic prices increased by 20%, the National Bank of Ukraine lost 40% of its gross reserves.

Uzbekistan

In the central Asian state, the government banned the free unlicensed sales of food, most of which is imported from Russia, as a preventative measure against price rises and panic.

CONCLUSION

It is seen that the Russian Financial Crisis started as a result of the Asian financial crisis. The Russian financial crisis has many economic and political effects as it has already been discussed in the chapter. To prevent the crisis the government of Russia employed the free float of its currency. But ultimately when the oil prices in the world started rising then Russia was able to manage its current account deficit and able to convert the deficit into a surplus. The crisis has a chain effect and it has affected many countries with which Russia was having trade relation. As a result of the crisis, these countries started to give a thought that they should not only dependent on Russia and they started finding other alternative partners for trade.

10 Argentine Economic Crisis

Overview of the Chapter
The chapter highlights the following important headings: • Origin of the Crisis • About the Crisis • End of Convertibility • Immediate Effects • Recovery • Debt Restructuring • Criticisms of IMF • Conclusion

The *Argentine Economic Crisis* was part of the situation that affected Argentina's economy during the late 1990s and early 2000s. Macro-economically speaking, the critical period started with the decrease of real GDP in 1999 and ended in 2002 with the return to GDP growth, but the origins of the collapse of Argentina's economy, and their effects on the population, can be found in action much before the crisis. As of 2005, arguably the crisis was over, though many challenges remain for the country like the unequal distribution of income and wealth etc.

ORIGIN OF THE CRISIS

Argentina was subject to military dictatorship (alternating with weak, short-lived democratic governments) for many years, which resulted in a number of significant economic problems. During the National Reorganization Process from 1976 to 1983 huge debt was acquired for money that was later lost in different unfinished projects, the Falklands War and the state's takeover of private debts. In this period, a neo liberal economic platform was introduced. By the end of the military government the country's industries were severely affected. The unemployment rate was calculated at 18% (though official figures claimed 5%). This was at its highest point since the depression.

In 1983, democracy in the country was restored with the election of President Raúl Alfonsín. The new government's plans included stabilizing Argentina's economy including the creation of a new currency (the *Austral*, first of its kind not to carry the word *peso* as part of its name), for which new loans were required. The state eventually became unable to pay the interest of this debt and confidence in the Austral collapsed. Inflation, which had been held to 10% to 20% a month, spiraled out of control. In July 1989, Argentina's inflation reached 200% that month alone, topping 5,000% for the year. During the Alfonsín years, unemployment did not substantially increase; but, real wages fell by almost half (to the lowest level in fifty years). Amid riots, President Alfonsín resigned five months before ending his term, and Carlos Menem took the office of the President.

Menem, who had campaigned on a populist platform, had a lukewarm start regarding the country's economy under ministers Miguel Ángel Roig (who died after a few days in office) and Antonio Erman Gonzalez, but then went back on his promises and began a plan, aligned on the neo liberal Washington consensus, of trade liberalization, labour deregulation and privatization of state companies which were the source of "much spending".

The fight against inflation did go well, and Argentina began to recover. In early 1991, under the rule of Minister of Economy Domingo Cavallo, executive measures fixed the value of Argentine currency at 10,000 Australes per United States dollar. Furthermore, any citizen could go to a bank and ask for any amount of cash in domestic currency to be converted to the corresponding amount of dollars; in order to secure this "convertibility", the Central Bank of Argentina was bound to keep its dollar foreign exchange reserves at the same level as the cash in circulation. The initial aim of such measures was to ensure the acceptance of domestic currency, since during 1989 and 1990 hyperinflation peaks; people had started to reject it as payment, demanding U.S. dollars instead. This regime was later fixated by a law (*Ley de Convertibilidad*) which restored the peso as the Argentine currency, with a monetary value fixed by law to the value of the United States dollar.

As a result of the convertibility law, inflation dropped sharply, price stability was assured, and the value of the currency was preserved. This raised the quality of life for many citizens, who could now afford to travel abroad, buy imported goods or ask for credits in dollars at very low interest rates.

But Argentina had international debts to pay, and it needed to keep borrowing money. The fixed exchange rate made imports cheap, producing a constant flight of dollars away from the country and a progressive loss of Argentina's industrial infrastructure, which led to an increase in unemployment.

In the meantime, government spending continued to be high and corruption was rampant. Argentina's public debt grew enormously during the 1990s, and the country showed no true signs of being able to pay it. The International Monetary Fund, however, kept lending money to Argentina and postponing its payment schedules. Massive tax evasion and money laundering explained a large part of the evaporation of funds toward offshore banks. A congressional committee started investigations in 2001 about accusations that the Central Bank of Argentina's governor, Pedro Pou, as well as part of the board of directors, had failed to investigate cases of alleged money laundering through Argentina's financial system. Clear stream was also accused of being instrumental in this global financial process.

Other countries, such as Mexico and Brazil (both of which also happen to be important trade partners for Argentina) faced economic crises of their own, leading other countries to mistrust Latin American countries money wise, and affecting the overall economy of the region. The influx of foreign currency provided by the privatization of state companies had dried out, and after 1999 Argentine exports were harmed by the devaluation of the Brazilian real and a considerable international revaluation of the dollar, effectively revaluing the peso against its major trading partners, Brazil (30% of total trade flows) and the euro area (23% of total trade flows).

By 1999, newly elected President Fernando de la Rúa faced a country where unemployment had risen to a critical point, and the undesirable effects of the fixed exchange rate were showing forcefully. In 1999 Argentina's GDP dropped 4% and the country entered a recession (which was to last three years, ending in a collapse). Economic stability became economic stagnation (even deflation at times), and the economic measures taken did nothing to avert it; in fact, the government continued the contractive economic policies of its predecessor. The possible solution (abandonment of the exchange peg, with a voluntary devaluation of the peso) was considered a political suicide and a recipe for economic disaster. By the end of the century, a spectrum of complementary currencies had emerged.

ABOUT THE CRISIS

Argentina quickly lost the confidence of investors and the flight of money away from the country increased. In 2001, people fearing the worst began withdrawing large sums of money from their bank accounts, turning pesos into dollars and sending them abroad, causing a run on the banks. The government then enacted a set of measures (informally known as the *corralito*) that effectively froze all bank accounts for twelve months, allowing for only minor sums of cash to be withdrawn.

Because of this allowance limit and the serious problems it caused in certain cases, many Argentines became enraged and took to the streets of important cities, especially Buenos Aires. They engaged in a form of popular protest that became known as *cacerolazo* (banging pots and pans). These protests occurred especially during the period of 2001 to 2002. At first the *cacerolazos* were simply noisy demonstrations, but soon they included property destruction, often directed at banks, foreign privatized companies, and especially big American and European companies. Many businesses installed metal barriers because windows and glass facades were being broken and even fires being ignited at their doors. Billboards of such companies as Coca Cola and others were brought down by the masses of demonstrators.

Confrontations between the police and citizens became a common sight, and fires were also set on Buenos Aires avenues. Fernando de la Rúa declared a state of emergency but this only worsened the situation, precipitating the violent protests of 20 and 21 December 2001 in Plaza de Mayo, where demonstrators clashed with the police, ended with several dead, and precipitated the fall of the government. De la Rúa eventually fled the Casa Rosada in a helicopter on 21 December, 2001.

Since De la Rúa's vice president, Carlos Álvarez, had resigned in October 2000, a political crisis ensued. Following presidential succession procedures established in the Constitution, the president of the Senate Ramón Puerta took office but quickly resigned, followed by the president of the Chamber of Deputies, Eduardo Camaño. The Legislative Assembly (a body formed by merging both chambers of the Congress) convened with the goal of creating a more legitimate interim government. By law, the candidates were its own members plus the Governors of the Provinces—they finally appointed Adolfo Rodríguez Saá, then governor of San Luis. During the last week of 2001, the interim government led by Rodríguez Saá, facing the impossibility of meeting debt payments, defaulted on the larger part of the public debt, totaling no less than 93 billion.

Politically, the most heated debate involved the time for the following elections—the spectrum ranged from March 2002 to October 2003 (the original date for the ending of De la Rúa's office).

Rodríguez Saá's economy team came up with a project designed to preserve the convertibility regime, dubbed the "Third Currency" Plan. It consisted of creating a new, non-convertible currency called *Argentino* coexisting with convertible pesos and U.S. dollars. It would only circulate as cash (checks, promisory notes or other instruments could be nominated in pesos or dollars but not in Argentinos) and would be partially guaranteed with federally-managed land - such features were expected to counterbalance inflationary tendencies.

Argentinos having legal currency status would be used to redeem all complementary currency already in circulation, the acceptance of which as a means of payment was quite uneven. It was hoped that preservation of convertibility would restore public confidence, while the non-convertible nature of this currency would allow for a measure of fiscal flexibility (unthinkable with pesos) that could ameliorate the crippling recession of economy. Critics called this plan merely a "controlled devaluation"; its advocates countered that since controlling devaluation is perhaps its thorniest issue, this criticism was praise in disguise. The "Third Currency" plan had enthusiastic supporters among mainstream economists. However, it could never be implemented because the Rodríguez Saá government lacked the political support required. Rodríguez Saá, utterly incapable to deal with the crisis and unsupported by his own party, resigned before the end of the year. The Legislative Assembly convened again, appointing Peronist Eduardo Duhalde—then a Senator for the Buenos Aires province—to take his place.

THE END OF CONVERTIBILITY

After much deliberation, Duhalde abandoned in January 2002 the fixed 1-to-1 peso-dollar parity that had been in place for ten years. In a matter of days, the peso lost a large part of its value in the unregulated market. A provisional "official" exchange rate was set at 1.4 pesos per dollar. In addition to the *corralito*, the Ministry of Economy dictated the *pesificación* ("peso-ification"), by which all bank accounts denominated in dollars would be converted to pesos at official rate. This measure angered most savings holders and appeals were made by many citizens to declare it unconstitutional.

After a few months, the exchange rate was left to float more or less freely. The peso suffered a huge depreciation, which in turn prompted inflation since Argentina depended heavily on imports, and had no means to replace them locally at the time.

The economic situation became steadily worse with regards to inflation and unemployment during 2002. By that time the original 1-to-1 rate had skyrocketed to nearly 4 pesos per dollar, while the accumulated inflation since the devaluation was about 80%.

Since the volume of pesos didn't fit the demand for cash (not even after the devaluation) huge quantities of a wide spectrum of complementary currency kept circulating alongside them. Fears of hyperinflation as a consequence of devaluation quickly eroded the attractiveness of their associated revenue, originally stated in convertible pesos. Their acceptability now ultimately depended on the State's willingness to take them as payment of taxes and other charges, consequently becoming very irregular. Very often they were taken at less than their nominal value—while the Patacón was frequently accepted at the same value as peso, Entre Ríos's *Federal* was among the worst-faring, at an average 30% as the provincial government that had issued them was reluctant to take them back. There were also frequent rumors that the Government would simply banish complementary currency overnight (instead of redeeming them, even at disadvantageous rates); leaving their holders with useless printed paper.

IMMEDIATE EFFECTS

Many private companies were affected by the crisis. Aerolíneas Argentinas, for example, was one of the most affected Argentine companies, having to stop all international flights for various days in 2002. The airline came close to bankruptcy, but survived. Most barter networks, viable as devices to ameliorate the shortage of cash during the recession, collapsed as large numbers of people turned to them, desperate to save as many pesos as they could for exchange for hard currency as a palliative for uncertainty.

Several thousand newly homeless and jobless Argentines found work as *cartoneros*, or cardboard collectors. The 2003 estimation of 30,000 to 40,000 people scavenged the streets for cardboard to eke out a living by selling it to recycling plants. This method accounts for only one of many ways of coping in a country that at the time suffered from an unemployment rate soaring at nearly 25%.

Agriculture was also affected. Argentine products were rejected in some international markets, in fear that they might come damaged because of the poor conditions in which they grew, and the USDA put restrictions on Argentine food and drugs arriving at the United States.

Producers of television channels were forced to produce more reality shows than any other type of shows, because these were generally cheap to produce as compared to other programmes. Virtually all education-related TV programmes were canceled.

Tourism balance with Chile inverted due to the lowered prices in Argentina.

THE RECOVERY

Eduardo Duhalde finally managed to stabilize the situation to a certain extent, and called for elections. On May 25, 2003 President Néstor Kirchner took charge. Kirchner kept Duhalde's Minister of Economy, Roberto Lavagna, in his post. Lavagna, a respected economist with centrist views, showed a considerable aptitude at managing the crisis, with the help of heterodox measures.

The economic outlook was completely different from that of the 1990s; the devalued peso made Argentine exports cheap and competitive abroad, while discouraging imports. In addition, the high price of soy in the international market produced an injection of massive amounts of foreign currency. The government encouraged import substitution and accessible credit for businesses, staged an aggressive plan to improve tax collection, and set aside large amounts of money for social welfare, while controlling expenditure in other fields. As a result of the administration's productive model and controlling measures (selling reserve dollars in the public market), the peso slowly revalued, reaching a 3-to-1 rate to the dollar. Agricultural exports grew and tourism returned.

The huge trade surplus ultimately caused such an inflow of dollars that the government was forced to begin intervening in order to keep the peso from revaluing further, which would have ruined the tax collection scheme (largely based on imports taxes and royalties) and discourage further reindustrialization. The central bank started buying dollars in the local market and stocking them as reserves. By December 2005, foreign currency reserves had reached $ 28 billion (they were greatly reduced by the anticipated payment of the full debt to the IMF in January 2006). The downside of this reserve accumulation strategy is that the dollars have to be bought with freshly-issued pesos, which may induce inflation. The central bank neutralizes a part of this monetary emission by selling Treasury letters. In this way the exchange rate has been stabilized near a reference value of 3 pesos to the dollar.

The currency exchange issue is complicated by two mutually opposing factors: a sharp increase in imports since 2004 (which raises the demand of dollars), and the return of foreign investment (which brings fresh currency from abroad) after the successful restructuring of about three quarters of the external debt. The government has set-up controls and restrictions aimed at keeping short-term speculative investment from destabilizing the financial market.

Argentina's recovery suffered a minor setback in 2004 when rising industrial demand caused a short-lived energy crisis.

Argentina has managed to return to growth with surprising strength; GNP jumped 8.8% in 2003, 9.0% in 2004, 9.2% in 2005, 8.5% in 2006 and 8.7% in 2007. Though average wages have increased 17% annually since 2002 (jumping 25% in the year to May 2008), consumer prices have partly accompanied this surge; though not comparable to the levels of former crises, the inflation rate was 12.5% in 2005, 10% in 2006 and is believed by private economists to have approached 15% in 2007 and to exceed 20% during 2008 This has prompted the government to increase tariffs for exporters and to pressure retailers into one price truce after another in a bid to stabilize prices, so far with little effect.

While unemployment has been considerably reduced (it's been hovering around 8.5% since 2006), Argentina has so far failed to reach an equitable distribution of income as the wealthiest 10% of the population receives 31 times more income than the poorest 10%.

During the economic collapse, many business owners and foreign investors drew all of their money out of the Argentine economy and sent it overseas. As a result, many small and medium enterprises closed due to lack of capital, thereby exacerbating unemployment. Many workers at these enterprises, faced with a sudden loss of employment and no source of income, decided to reopen businesses on their own, without the presence of the owners and their capital, as self-managed cooperatives. Worker managed cooperative businesses range from ceramics factory Zanon (FaSinPat), to the four-star Hotel Bauen, to suit factory Brukman, to printing press Chilavert, and many others. As of 2007, there were about 10,000 people employed in self-managed businesses, representing a significant source of employment and economic growth. In some cases, the former owners sent police to kick workers out of the workplaces; this was sometimes successful but in other cases workers defended occupied workplaces against the state, the police, and the bosses.

Some businesses have now been legally purchased by the workers for nominal fees, others remain 'occupied' by workers who have no legal standing with the state (and in some cases reject negotiation with the state on the grounds that working productively is its own justification). The Argentine government is considering a Law of Expropriation that would transfer some occupied businesses to their worker-managers.

DEBT RESTRUCTURING

When the default was declared in 2002, foreign investment fled the country, and capital flow towards Argentina ceased almost completely. The Argentine government met severe challenges trying to refinance the debt. The state had no spare money at the time, and the central bank's foreign currency reserves were almost depleted.

The Argentine government kept a firm stance, and finally got a deal in 2005 by which 76% of the defaulted bonds were exchanged by others, of a much lower nominal value (25–35%

of the original) and at longer terms. In 2008, President Cristina Fernandez de Kirchner announced she was studying a reopening of the 2005 swap in order to gain adhesion from the remaining 24% of the so-called "holdouts," and thereby fully exit the default with private investors.

CRITICISM OF THE IMF

The International Monetary Fund suffered no discounts in its part of the Argentine debt. Some payments were refinanced or postponed on agreement. However, the authorities of the IMF at times expressed harsh criticism of the discounts and actively lobbied for the private creditors.

In a speech before the United Nations General Assembly on September 21, 2004, President Kirchner said that "An urgent, tough, and structural redesign of the International Monetary Fund is needed, to prevent crises and help in [providing] solutions". Implicitly referencing the fact that the intent of the original Bretton Woods system was to encourage economic development, Kirchner warned that the IMF today must "change that direction which took it from being a lender for development to a creditor demanding privileges".

In 2005, as a large and consistently growing fiscal surplus made it possible, Argentina shifted to a policy of "disindebtment" towards the IMF by paying the IMF in schedule, with no negotiation whenever possible, with the intention of gaining independence from it. On December 15, 2005, in a sudden move following Brazil, President Kirchner announced that Argentina would pay the whole debt to the IMF which had been previously financed in instalments until 2008, for a total of 9,810 million USD, employing the central bank's foreign currency reserves.

In a report published in June 2006, a group of independent experts hired by the IMF to revise the work of its Independent Evaluation Office (IEO) stated that the assessment of the Argentine case suffered from informative manipulation and lack of collaboration on the part of the IMF; the IEO is claimed to have unduly softened its conclusions to avoid criticizing the IMF's board of directors.

CONCLUSION

It was because of the Argentine Economic Crisis the quality of life of the average Argentinian was lowered proportionally; many businesses closed or went bankrupt, many imported products became virtually inaccessible, and salaries were left as they were before the crisis. This crisis has brought another innovation as many workers during that time were jobless and no source of income, decided to reopen businesses on their own, without the presence of the owners and their capital, as self-managed cooperatives. Later on due to the heavy de-valuation of the Argentine currency the export boosted and import was expensive hence the trade surplus of the country grown up considerably, and several measures taken up by the government including the restructuring of the debt which helped Argentina to come out of the crisis. But still the cause of the concern for the policy-makers is the unequal distribution of the wealth in Argentina.

11 Burst of Dot-Com Bubble

Overview of the Chapter

The present chapter throws a light on the burst of the dot com bubble. It happened during the early part of the 21st century. The contents of the chapter are as follows:

- The Growth of the Bubble
- The beginning of the Crash
- Consequences of the Crash
- Companies Significant to the Bubble
- Conclusion

The *"dot-com bubble"* which is also known as the *"I.T. bubble"* was a speculative bubble covering roughly 1995-2001 (with a climax on March 10, 2000 with the NASDAQ peaking at 5132.52). During this period the stock markets in Western nations saw their value increase rapidly from growth in the new internet sector and related fields. The period was marked by the founding (and, in many cases, spectacular failure) of a group of new Internet-based companies commonly referred to as *dot-coms*. A combination of rapidly increasing stock prices, individual speculation in stocks, and widely available venture capital created an exuberant environment in which many of these businesses dismissed standard business models, focusing on increasing market share at the expense of the bottom line.

THE GROWTH OF THE BUBBLE

The venture capitalists saw record-setting rises in stock valuations of *dot-com* companies, and therefore moved faster and with less caution than usual, choosing to mitigate the risk by starting many contenders and letting the market decide which would succeed. The low interest rates in 1998–99 helped increase the start-up capital amounts. Although a number of these new entrepreneurs had realistic plans and administrative ability, many more of them lacked these characteristics but were able to sell their ideas to investors because of the novelty of the dot-com concept.

A canonical "dot-com" company's business model relied on harnessing network effects by operating at a sustained net loss to build market share (or mind share). These companies expected that they could build enough brand awareness to charge profitable rates for their services later. The motto "get big fast" reflected this strategy. During the loss period, the companies relied on venture capital and especially initial public offerings of stock to pay their expenses. The novelty of these stocks, combined with the difficulty of valuing the companies, sent many stocks to dizzying heights and made the initial controllers of the company wildly rich on paper.

Historically, the dot-com boom can be seen as similar to a number of other technology-inspired booms of the past including railroads in the 1840s, automobiles and radio in the 1920s, transistor electronics in the 1950s, computer time-sharing in the 1960s, and home computers and biotechnology in the early 1980s in accordance with the Japanese economic meltdown.

Soaring Stocks

A stock market bubble is a self-perpetuating rise or boom in the share prices of stocks of a particular industry. The term may be used with certainty only in retrospect when share prices have since crashed. A bubble occurs when speculators note the fast increase in value and decide to buy in anticipation of further rises, rather than because the shares are undervalued. Typically many companies thus become grossly overvalued. When the bubble "bursts," the share prices fall dramatically, and many companies go out of business.

The dot-com model was inherently flawed. A vast number of companies had the same business plan of monopolizing their respective sectors through network effects, and it was clear that even if the plan was sound, there could only be at most one network-effects winner in each sector, and therefore that most companies with this business plan would fail. In fact, many sectors could not support even one company powered entirely by network effects.

In spite of this, however, a few company founders made vast fortunes when their companies were bought out at an early stage in the dot-com stock market bubble. These early successes made the bubble even more buoyant. An unprecedented amount of personal investing occurred during the boom, and many of the news papers reported the phenomenon of people quitting their jobs to become full-time day traders.

Free Spending

According to dot-com theory, an Internet company's survival depend on expanding its customer base as rapidly as possible, even if it produced large annual losses. For instance, Google and Amazon did not see any profit in their first years. Amazon was spending on expanding customer base and letting people know that it existed and Google was busy spending on creating more powerful machine capacity to serve its expanding search engine. The phrase "Get large or get lost" was the wisdom of the day. At the height of the boom, it was possible for a promising dot-com to make an initial public offering (IPO) of its stock and raise a substantial amount of money even though it had never made a profit or, in some cases, earned some revenue somehow. In such a situation, a company's lifespan was measured by its burn rate, that is, the rate at which a non-profitable company lacking a viable business model ran through its capital served as the metric.

Public awareness campaigns were one way that dot-coms sought to grow their customer base. These included television ads, print ads, and targeting of professional sporting events. Many dot-coms named themselves with onomatopoeic nonsense words that they hoped would be memorable and not easily confused with a competitor. Super Bowl XXXIV in January 2000 featured seventeen dot-com companies that each paid over two million dollars for a thirty-second spot. By contrast, in January 2001, just *three* dot-coms bought advertising spots during Super Bowl XXXV. In a similar vein, CBS-backed iWon.com gave away ten million dollars to a lucky contestant on an April 15, 2000, half-hour primetime special that was broadcast on CBS.

Not surprisingly, the "growth over profits" mentality and the aura of "new economy" invincibility led some companies to engage in lavish internal spending, such as elaborate business facilities and luxury vacations for employees. Executives and employees who were paid with stock options in lieu of cash became instant millionaires when the company made its initial public offering; many invested their new wealth into yet more dot-coms.

Cities all over the United States sought to become the "next Silicon Valley" by building network-enabled office space to attract Internet entrepreneurs. Communication providers, convinced that the future economy would require ubiquitous broadband access, went deeply into debt to improve their networks with high-speed equipment and fiber optic cables. Companies that produced network equipment, such as Cisco Systems, profited greatly from these projects.

Similarly, in Europe the vast amounts of cash the mobile operators spent on 3G licenses in Germany, Italy, and the United Kingdom, for example, led them into deep debt. The investments were far out of proportion to both their current and projected cash flow, but this was not publicly acknowledged until as late as 2001 and 2002. Due to the highly networked nature of the IT (information-technology) industry, this quickly led to problems for small companies dependent on contracts from operators.

THE CRASH BEGINS

During the late 1999 and early 2000, the Federal Reserve

had increased interest rates six times, and the runaway economy was beginning to lose speed. The dot-com bubble burst, numerically, on March 10, 2000, when the technology heavy NASDAQ Composite index peaked at 5,048.62 (intra-day peak 5,132.52), more than double its value just a year before. The NASDAQ fell slightly after that, but this was attributed to correction by most market analysts; the actual reversal and subsequent bear market may have been triggered by the adverse findings of fact in the *United States v. Microsoft* case which was being heard in federal court. The findings, which declared Microsoft a monopoly, were widely expected in the weeks before their release on April 3, 2000.

One possible cause for the collapse of the NASDAQ (and all dotcoms) was massive, multi-billion dollar sell orders for major bellwether high tech stocks (Cisco, IBM, Dell, etc.) that happened by chance to be processed simultaneously on the Monday morning following the March 10, 2000 weekend. This selling resulted in the NASDAQ opening roughly four percentage points lower on Monday March 13, 2000 from 5,038 to 4,879. It was the greatest percentage 'pre-market' sell-off for the entire year.

The massive initial batch of sell orders processed on Monday, March 13, 2000 triggered a chain reaction of selling that fed on itself as investors, funds, and institutions liquidated positions. In just six days the NASDAQ had lost nearly nine percent, falling from roughly 5,050 on March 10, 2000 to 4,580 on March 15, 2000.

Another reason may have been accelerated business spending in preparation for the Y2K switchover. Once New Year had passed without incident, businesses found themselves with all the equipment they needed for some time, and business spending quickly declined. This correlates quite closely to the peak of U.S. stock markets. The Dow Jones peaked on January 14, 2000 (closed at 11,722.98, with an intra-day peak of 11,750.28 and theoretical peak of 11,908.50) and the broader SandP 500 on March 24, 2000 (closed at 1,527.46, with an intra-day peak of 1,553.11); while, even more dramatically the UK's FTSE 100 Index peaked at 6,950.60 on the last day of trading in 1999 (December 30). Hiring freezes, layoffs, and consolidations followed in several industries, especially in the dot-com sector.

The bursting of the bubble may also have been related to the poor results of Internet retailers following the 1999 Christmas season. This was the first unequivocal and public evidence that the "Get Rich Quick" Internet strategy was flawed for most companies. These retailers' results were made public in March when annual and quarterly reports of public firms were released.

By 2001, the bubble was deflating at full speed. A majority of the dot-coms ceased trading after burning through their venture capital, many having never made a net profit. Investors often jokingly referred to these failed dot-coms as either "dot-bombs" or "dot-compost".

CONSEQUENCES OF THE BURST

On January 11, 2000, America Online, a favourite of dot-com investors and pioneer of dial-up Internet access, acquired Time Warner, the world's largest media company. Within two years, boardroom disagreements drove out both of the CEOs who made the deal, and in October 2003 *AOL Time Warner* dropped "AOL" from its name, a symbol of the dominance of old industry during periods of technological growth.

Several communication companies, burdened with unredeemable debts from their expansion projects, sold their assets for cash or filed for bankruptcy. WorldCom, the largest of these, was found to have used illegal accounting practices to overstate its profits by billions of dollars. The company's stock crashed when these irregularities were revealed, and within days it filed the second largest corporate bankruptcy in U.S. history. Other examples include North Point Communications, Global Crossing, JDS Uniphase, XO Communications, and Covad Communications. Demand for the new high-speed infrastructure never materialized, and it became dark fiber, impacting companies such as Nortel, Cisco and Corning, whose stock plunged from a high of $ 113 to a low of $ 1.

Many dot-coms ran out of capital and were acquired or liquidated; the domain names were picked up by old-economy competitors or domain name investors. Several companies and their executives were accused or convicted of fraud for misusing shareholders' money, and the U.S. Securities and Exchange Commission (SEC) fined top investment firms like Citigroup and Merrill Lynch millions of dollars for misleading investors. Various supporting industries, such as advertising and shipping, scaled back their operations as demand for their services fell. A few large dot-com companies, such as Amazon.com and eBay, survived the turmoil and appear assured of long-term survival.

The dot-com bubble crash wiped out $ 5 trillion in market value of technology companies from March 2000 to October 2002.

Recent research suggests, however, that as many as 50% of the dot-coms survived through 2004, reflecting two facts: the destruction of public market wealth did not necessarily correspond to firm closings, and second, that most of the dot-coms were small players who were able to weather the financial markets storm.

Nevertheless, laid-off technology experts, such as computer programmers, found a glutted job market. In the U.S., International outsourcing and the recently allowed increase of skilled visa "guest workers" (e.g., those participating in the U.S. H-1B visa program) exacerbated the situation. University degree programs for computer-related careers saw a noticeable drop in new students. Anecdotes of unemployed programmers going back to school to become accountants or lawyers were common.

Some believe the crash of the dot-com bubble contributed to the housing bubble in the U.S. Yale economist Robert Shiller said in 2005, "Once stocks fell, real estate became the primary outlet for the speculative frenzy that the stock market had unleashed. Where else could plungers apply their newly acquired trading talents? The materialistic display of the big house also has become a salve to bruised egos of disappointed stock investors. These days, the only thing that comes close to real estate as a national obsession is poker."

COMPANIES SIGNIFICANT TO BUBBLE

Given below is the list of some of the important IT

companies who were severely hit by the bubble. However, the list is not exhaustive.

- Boo.com, spent $ 188 million in just six months in an attempt create a global online fashion store. Went bankrupt in May 2000.
- Boxman AB, Pan-European online retailer of home entertainment with ambition of becoming the European amazon.com. Bankrupt in November 2000.
- E-Digital Corporation, (EDIG): OTCE B stock that went from closing price of $ 2.91 on 12/31/99 to intraday high of $ 24.50 on 1/24/00. It quickly retraced and has traded below $ 0.29 since 2006.
- eToys, share price went from the $ 80 reached during its IPO in May 1999 to less than $ 1 when it declared bankruptcy in February 2001.
- Freeinternet.com—Filed for bankruptcy in October 2000, soon after canceling its IPO. At the time Freeinternet.com was the fifth largest ISP in the United States, with 3.2 million users. Famous for its mascot Baby Bob, the company lost $ 19 million in 1999 on revenues of less than $ 1 million.
- GeoCities, purchased by Yahoo! for $ 3.57 billion in January 1999.
- Hotmail—founder Sabeer Bhatia sold the company to Microsoft for $ 400 million; at that time Hotmail had 9 million members.
- Inktomi-stock peaked at $ 241 a share (split adjusted) in March 2000. The company was sold to Yahoo! in 2002 for $ 1.63 a share.
- K-tel—In 1998, the company's stock shot from about $ 3 in April to around $ 34 in early May but eventually declined to pennies by 1999.
- InfoSpace—In March 2000 this stock reached a price $ 1,305 per share, but by April 2001 its price had crashed down to $ 22 a share.
- Kozmo.com, shut down in April 2001, featured in the documentary film *e-Dreams*.
- Kibu.com, shut down in October 2000.

- The Learning Company, bought by Mattel in 1999 for $ 3.5 billion, sold for $ 27.3 million in 2000.
- Mortgage.com, formerly 1st Mortgage Network spun off Mortgage Systems International (MSI).. ABN Amro Mortgage Group purchased the domain, and moved National Lending Center from Ann Arbor Michigan to take over the lease in the "White Elephant" building in Sunrise Florida. ABN Amro Mortgage Group has been since purchased by CitiMortgage Group in March 2007.
- Nortel Networks, a prominent Canadian company whose shares fell from C$ 124 to $ 0.47. On Jan. 14-09 it filed for bankruptcy protection, and stocks fell 75% in after-hour trading to 0.075$ a share.
- PayPal, now a subsidiary of eBay.
- theGlobe.com, set a record for one-day share price gain (606%) on its IPO, hitting $ 97; shares now trade for less than a nickel.
- Think Tools AG, one of the most extreme symptoms of the bubble in Europe: market valuation of CHF 2.5 billion in March 2000, no prospects of having a substantial product (investor deception), followed by a collapse.
- Webvan: This grocery delivery service spent too much on infrastructure (close to $ 1 billion) before it had even turned a profit. Went bankrupt in 2001.
- WorldCom, at one time controlled a majority of U.S. Internet backbone, through acquisition of UUNet and MCI; acquired by Verizon after financial scandal.
- Yahoo!: Went from high of $ 128 at the peak of bubble to $ 4 at the end of the bubble.

CONCLUSION

It is observed in the above paragraphs that the world wide stock market crash of 2000-01 was the result of the burst of the IT bubble created during that year. Due to the increase in the interest rate and not coming of the results of these companies upto the expectations of the investors the bubble burst. The impact of the bubble was world wide. And millions of the investors have lost their money. The burst of the IT bubble have again put an example before the world that if any thing's growth is not properly backed by the strong fundamentals it is difficult to sustain the growth in the long-run and in the long run only the natural growth which is supported by the fundamentals will sustain.

Global Financial Crisis of 2008-09

The *global financial crisis of 2008-09* is the recent financial crisis the world has faced. It became prominently visible in September 2008 with the failure, merger, or conservatorship of several large United States-based financial firms. The underlying causes leading to the crisis had been reported in business journals, magazines and news papers for many months before September 2008, with commentary about the financial stability of leading U.S. and European investment banks, insurance firms and mortgage banks consequent to the sub-prime mortgage crisis.

Overview of the Chapter

The present chapter highlights the ongoing global financial crisis of the world. Till the writing of this chapter the crisis was not finished. The chapter highlights the following important headings:

- Introduction to the Crisis
- The Month of September, 2008
- The Month of October, 2008
- The Month of November, 2008
- The Month of December, 2008
- The Month of January, 2009
- Global Response to the Crisis
- Conclusion

The crisis begins with the failures of large financial institutions in the United States. It rapidly evolved into a global credit crisis. It also resulted in deflation and sharp reductions in shipping which results in a number of European bank failures and declines in various stock indexes, and large reductions in the market value of equities (stock) and commodities worldwide. The credit crisis was exacerbated by Section 128 of the Emergency Economic Stabilization Act of 2008 which allowed the Federal Reserve System to pay interest on excess reserve requirement balances held on deposit from banks, removing the longstanding incentive for banks to extend credit instead of hoard cash on deposit with the Fed. The crisis led to a liquidity problem and the de-leveraging of financial institutions especially in the United States and Europe, which further accelerated the liquidity crisis, and a decrease in international shipping and commerce. World political leaders and national ministers of finance and central bank directors have coordinated their efforts to reduce fears but the crisis was ongoing and continues to change, evolving at the close of October into a currency crisis with investors transferring vast capital resources into stronger currencies such as the yen, the dollar and the Swiss franc, leading many emergent economies to seek aid from the International Monetary Fund. The crisis was triggered by the sub prime mortgage crisis and is an acute phase of the financial crisis of 2007–09.

INTRODUCTION TO THE CRISIS

The sub-prime mortgage crisis reached a critical stage during the first week of September 2008. It was characterized by severely contracted liquidity in the global credit markets and insolvency threats to investment banks and other institutions.

Reserve balances from banks in the Federal Reserve System began increasing over required levels of about $ 10 billion at the beginning of September 2008, just after the Democratic and Republican national conventions, and just before the stock market crash and presidential debates. Beginning October 6, Section 128 of the Emergency Economic

Stabilization Act of 2008 allowed the Federal Reserve System to pay interest on the excess balances, producing further pressure on international credit markets. Excess on reserve balances topped $ 870 billion by the end of the second week of January 2009. In comparison, the increase in reserve balances reached only $ 65 billion after September 11, 2001 before falling back to normal levels within a month.

Government Takeover of Home Mortgage Lenders

The director of the Federal Housing Finance Agency (FHFA), in United States James B. Lockhart III, on September 7, 2008 announced his decision to place two United States Government sponsored enterprises (GSEs), Fannie Mae (Federal National Mortgage Association) and Freddie Mac (Federal Home Loan Mortgage Corporation), into conservatorship run by FHFA. United States Treasury Secretary Henry Paulson, at the same press conference stated that placing the two GSEs into conservatorship was a decision he fully supported, and said that he advised *"that conservatorship was the only form in which I would commit taxpayer money to the GSEs."* He further said that *"I attribute the need for today's action primarily to the inherent conflict and flawed business model embedded in the GSE structure, and to the ongoing housing correction."* The same day, Federal Reserve Bank Chairman Ben Bernanke stated in support, *"I strongly endorse both the decision by FHFA Director Lockhart to place Fannie Mae and Freddie Mac into conservatorship and the actions taken by Treasury Secretary Paulson to ensure the financial soundness of those two companies."*

Major Financial Firm Crisis

On Sunday, September 14, 2008 it was announced that Lehman Brothers would file for bankruptcy after the Federal Reserve Bank declined to participate in creating a financial support facility for Lehman Brothers. The significance of the Lehman Brothers bankruptcy is disputed with some assigning it a pivotal role in the unfolding of subsequent events. The principals involved, Ben Bernanke and Henry Paulson, dispute this view, citing a volume of toxic assets at Lehman which made a rescue impossible. Immediately following the bankruptcy, JP Morgan Chase provided the broker dealer unit of Lehman Brothers with $ 138 billion to "settle securities transactions with customers of Lehman and its clearance parties" according to a statement made in a New York City Bankruptcy court filing.

The same day, the sale of Merrill Lynch to Bank of America was announced. The beginning of the week was marked by extreme instability in global stock markets, with dramatic drops in market values on Monday, September 15, 2008 and Wednesday, September 17, 2008. On September 16, 2008 the large insurer American International Group (AIG), a significant participant in the credit default swaps markets suffered a liquidity crisis following the downgrade of its credit rating. The Federal Reserve, at AIG's request, and after AIG has shown that it could not find lenders willing to save it from insolvency, created a credit facility for up to US$ 85 billion in exchange for a 79.9% equity interest, and the right to suspend dividends to previously issued common and preferred stock.

Money Market Funds Insurance and Short Sales Prohibitions

On September 16, 2008, the Reserve Primary Fund, a large money market mutual fund, lowered its share price below $ 1 because of exposure to Lehman debt securities. This resulted in demands from investors to return their funds as the financial crisis mounted. By the morning of September 18, 2008, money market sell orders from institutional investors totalled $ 0.5 trillion, out of a total market capitalization of $ 4 trillion, but a $ 105 billion liquidity injection from the Federal Reserve averted an immediate collapse. On September 19, 2008, the U.S. Treasury offered temporary insurance (akin to FDIC insurance of bank accounts) to money market funds. Toward the end of the week, short selling of financial stocks was suspended by the Financial Services Authority (FSA) in the United Kingdom and by the Securities and Exchange Commission (SEC) in the United States. Similar measures were taken by authorities in other countries. Some restoration of market confidence occurred with the publicity surrounding efforts of the Treasury and the Securities Exchange Commission.

Troubled Asset Relief Program

On September 19, 2008 a plan intended to ameliorate the difficulties caused by the sub-prime mortgage crisis was proposed by the Secretary of the Treasury, Henry Paulson. He proposed a Troubled Assets Relief Program (TARP), later incorporated into the Emergency Economic Stabilization Act, which would permit the United States government to purchase illiquid assets, informally termed *toxic assets*, from financial institutions. The value of the securities was extremely difficult to determine.

Consultations between the Secretary of the Treasury, the Chairman of the Federal Reserve, and the Chairman of the SEC, Congressional leaders and the President of the United States moved forward plans to advance a comprehensive solution to the problems created by illiquid mortgage-backed securities. At the close of the week, the Secretary of the Treasury and President Bush announced a proposal for the federal government to buy up to US $ 700 billion of illiquid mortgage backed securities with the intent to increase the liquidity of the secondary mortgage markets and reduce potential losses encountered by financial institutions owning the securities. The draft proposal of the plan was received favorably by investors in the stock market.

THE MONTH OF SEPTEMBER, 2008

Week of September 21, 2008

On Sunday, September 21, 2008, the two remaining investment banks, Goldman Sachs and Morgan Stanley, with the approval of the Federal Reserve, converted to bank holding companies, a status subject to more regulation, but with readier access to capital. On September 21, 2008, Treasury Secretary Henry Paulson announced that the original proposal, which would have excluded foreign banks, had been widened to include foreign financial institutions with a presence in the US. The US administration was pressuring other countries to set up similar bailout plans.

On Monday and Tuesday, during the week of September 22, 2008, appearances were made by the Secretary of the Treasury and the Chairman of the Board of Governors of the

Federal Reserve before Congressional committees and on Wednesday a prime-time presidential address was delivered by the President of the United States on television. Behind the scenes, negotiations were held refining the proposal which had grown to 42 pages from its original 3 and was reported to include both an oversight structure and limitations on executive salaries, with other provisions under consideration.

On September 25, 2008, agreement was reported by congressional leaders on the basics of the package; however, general and vocal opposition to the proposal was voiced by the public. On Thursday afternoon at a White House meeting attended by congressional leaders and the presidential candidates, John McCain and Barack Obama, it became clear that there was no congressional consensus, with Republican representatives and the ranking member of the Senate Banking Committee, Richard C. Shelby, strongly opposing the proposal. The alternative advanced by conservative House Republicans was to create a system of mortgage insurance funded by fees on those holding mortgages; as the working week ended, negotiations continued on the plan, which had grown to 102 pages and included mortgage insurance as an option. On Thursday evening Washington Mutual, the nation's largest savings and loan, was seized by the Federal Deposit Insurance Corporation and most of its assets transferred to JP Morgan Chase. Wachovia, one of the largest US banks, was reported to be in negotiations with Citigroup and other financial institutions.

Week of September 28, 2008

Early into Sunday morning an announcement was made by the United States Secretary of the Treasury and congressional leaders that agreement had been reached on all major issues. The total amount of $ 700 billion remained with provision for the option of creating a scheme of mortgage insurance.

It was reported on Sunday, September 28, 2008, that a rescue plan had been crafted for the British mortgage lender Bradford and Bingley. Grupo Santander, the largest bank in Spain, was slated to take over the offices and savings accounts while the mortgage and loans business would be nationalized.

Fortis, a huge Benelux banking and finance company was partially nationalized on September 28, 2008, with Belgium, the Netherlands and Luxembourg investing a total of €11.2 billion (US$ 16.3 billion) in the bank. Belgium will purchase 49% of Fortis's Belgian division, with the Netherlands doing the same for the Dutch division. Luxembourg has agreed to a loan convertible into a 49% share of Fortis's Luxembourg division.

It was reported on Monday morning, September 29, 2008, which Wachovia, the 4th largest bank in the United States, would be acquired by Citigroup.

On Monday the German finance minister announced a rescue of Hypo Real Estate, a Munich-based holding company comprised of a number of real estate financing banks, but the deal collapsed on Saturday, October 4, 2008.

The same day the government of Iceland nationalized Glitnir, Iceland's third largest lender.

Stocks fell dramatically Monday in Europe and the US despite infusion of funds into the market for short-term credit. In the US the Dow-Jones dropped 777 points (6.98%), the largest one-day point-drop in history (but only the 17th largest percentage drop).

The U.S. bailout plan, now named the Emergency Economic Stabilization Act of 2008 and expanded to 110 pages was slated for consideration in the House of Representatives on Monday, September 29, 2008 as HR 3997 and in the Senate later in the week. The plan failed after the vote being held open for 40 minutes in the House of Representatives, 205 for the plan, 228 against. Meanwhile US stock markets suffered steep declines, the Dow-Jones losing 300 points in a matter of minutes, ending down 777.68, the NASDAQ losing 199.61, falling below the 2000 point mark, and the SandP. 500 off 8.77% for the day. By the end of the day, the Dow-Jones suffered the largest drop in the history of the index. The SandP 500 Banking Index fell 14% on September 29, 2008 with drops in the stock value of a number of US banks generally considered sound, including Bank of New York Mellon, State Street and Northern Trust; three Ohio banks, National City, Fifth Third, and Key Bank were down dramatically.

On Tuesday, September 30, 2008, stocks rebounded but credit markets remained tight with the London Inter-bank Offered Rate (overnight dollar Libor) rising 4.7% to 6.88%.

On Tuesday, September 30, 2008, 9 billion was made available by the French, Belgian and Luxembourg governments to the French-Belgian bank Dexia.

After Irish banks came under pressure on Monday, September 29, 2008, the Irish government undertook a two year "guarantee arrangement to safeguard all deposits (retail, commercial, institutional and inter-bank), covered bonds, senior debt and dated subordinated debt (lower tier II)" of 6 Irish banks: Allied Irish Banks, Bank of Ireland, Anglo Irish Bank, Irish Life and Permanent, Irish Nationwide and the EBS Building Society; the potential liability involved is about 400 billion dollars.

Key Risk Indicators in September

Key risk indicators became highly volatile during September 2008, a factor leading the U.S. government to pass the Emergency Economic Stabilization Act of 2008. The "TED spread" is a measure of credit risk for inter-bank lending. It is the difference between: (1) the risk-free three-month U.S. Treasury bill rate; and (2) the three-month London Inter Bank Offered Rate (LIBOR), which represents the rate at which banks typically lend to each other. A higher spread indicates banks perceive each other as riskier counterparties. The t-bill is considered "risk-free" because the full faith and credit of the U.S. government is behind it; theoretically, the government could just print money so that the principal is fully repaid at maturity. The TED spread reached record levels in late September 2008. The diagram indicates that the Treasury yield movement was a more significant driver than the changes in LIBOR. A three month t-bill yield so close to zero means that people are willing to forgo interest just to keep their money (principal) safe for three months—a very high level of risk aversion and indicative of tight lending conditions. Driving this change were investors shifting funds from money market funds (generally considered nearly risk free but paying a slightly higher rate of return than t-bills) and other investment types to t-bills. These issues are consistent with the September

2008 aspects of the subprime mortgage crisis which prompted the Emergency Economic Stabilization Act of 2008 signed into law by the U.S. President on October 2, 2008.

In addition, an increase in London Inter Bank Offer Rate [LIBOR] means that financial instrument with variable interest terms is increasingly expensive. Some estimate as much as $ 150 trillion in loans and derivatives are tied to LIBOR. Furthermore, the basis swap between one-month LIBOR and three-month LIBOR increased from 30 basis points in the beginning of September to a high of over 100 basis points. Financial institutions with liability exposure to 1 month LIBOR but funding from 3 month LIBOR faced increased funding costs. Higher interest rates place additional downward pressure on consumption, increasing the risk of recession.

THE MONTH OF OCTOBER, 2008

Beginning of October 2008

The United States Senate's version of the $ 700 billion bailout plan, modified to expand bank deposit guarantees to $ 250,000 and to include $ 100 billion in tax breaks for businesses and alternative energy, passed with bi-partisan support on October 1st, 2008. Reaction in the House was mixed, but in a vote on Friday the House of Representatives passed the Emergency Economic Stabilization Act of 2008, as refashioned by the Senate, in a bipartisan vote.

Discussions were ongoing in Europe regarding possible remedies for financial instability in Europe leading up to a conference Saturday afternoon in Paris hosted by Nicolas Sarkozy, president of France. Uni-Credit of Italy was reported to be the latest bank to come under pressure. During the night of October 2, 2008, Greece followed Ireland's lead and guaranteed all bank deposits.

On October 3, 2008, it was reported that Wachovia had rejected the previous offer from Citigroup in favour of acquisition by Wells Fargo, resulting in a legal dispute with Citigroup.

In Britain, the FSA announced on October 3, 2008, that effective from Tuesday, October 7, 2008, the amount of the guarantee of bank deposits would be raised to £ 50,000 from

£ 35,000. On Friday, October 3, 2008, the government of the Netherlands took over the Dutch operations of Fortis. It replaces the bailout plan of September 28, 2008.

Over the weekend and on Monday a major banking and financial crisis emerged in Iceland with its currency the Krona which dropped by 30% against the euro. At a meeting on Monday night emergency legislation was passed granting broad powers to the government to seize and regulate banks. On October 6, 2008, the Icelandic Financial Supervisory Authority decided temporarily to suspend from trading on regulated markets all financial instruments issued by different financial institution.

Before the opening of the business day on October 6, 2008, BNP Paribas, the French bank, assumed control of the remaining assets of Fortis following Dutch nationalization of the operations of the bank in The Netherlands. Denmark, Austria, and possibly Germany, joined Ireland and Greece in guaranteeing bank deposits on Monday, October 6. Following this, the FTSE100 index of leading British shares had its largest one-day points fall since it was established in 1984. A banking Bill easing rescues is slated for introduction in the British Parliament on Tuesday, October 7, 2008. On October 6, German chancellor Angela Merkel pledged that the government would guarantee all German private bank savings. The government also announced a revised bailout plan for German mortgage lender Hypo Real Estate (HRE). On Monday, October 6, the Dow Jones Industrial Average closed below 10,000, a drop of 30% from its high above 14,000 a year earlier on October 9, 2007. In Brazil and Russia trading was suspended on Monday following dramatic drops in their markets.

On October 7, 2008, the Central Bank of Iceland announced that Russia had agreed to provide a €4 billion loan, however this was soon denied by Russian authorities, and the Icelandic Finance Minister had to correct the earlier announcement and then stated that discussions had been initiated with Russia on providing a loan to Iceland. This was also denied by Russian Deputy Finance Minister Dmitry Pankin. Late in the evening, however, Russia's Finance Minister Alexei Kudrin did concede that a request had been received, to which Russia was positive, and that discussions on financial matters would be conducted later in the week when an Icelandic delegation was expected to arrive in Moscow. Standard and Poor's also cut Iceland's foreign-currency sovereign credit rating from A-/A-2 to BBB/A-3 and local-currency sovereign credit rating from A+/A-1 to BBB+/A-2. SandP also lowered Iceland's banking industry country risk assessment from group 5 to group 8, worrying that "In a severe recession scenario, the cumulative amount of non-performing and restructured loans could reach 35% to 50% of total outstanding loans in Iceland.

On October 7, 2008, the Federal Reserve announced formation of a Commercial Paper Funding Facility (CPFF) which was expected to serve as a funding backstop to facilitate the issuance of term commercial paper by eligible issuers. Several countries announced new or increased deposit guarantees. Taiwan outlined plans to double the guarantee to NT$ 3 million ($ 92,000) and the European Union agreed to increase guarantees across the EU to at least € 50,000 per saver. Several EU states then announced increases on top of this minimum.

The government of Britain announced on the morning of Wednesday, October 8, 2008, that it would make £ 25 billion available as "Tier 1 capital" to the following financial institutions: Abbey, Barclays, HBOS, HSBC Bank plc, Lloyds TSB, Nationwide Building Society, Royal Bank of Scotland, and Standard Chartered as part of a bank rescue package. An additional £ 25 billion was scheduled to be made available to other financial institutions, including British subsidiaries of foreign banks. The plan included increased ability to borrow from the government, offered assistance in raising equity, and a statement of support for international efforts. The plan has been described as partial nationalization.

On Wednesday, October 8, 2008, the European Central Bank, Bank of England, Federal Reserve, Bank of Canada, Swedish Riksbank and Swiss National Bank all announced simultaneous cuts of 0.5% to their base rates. Shortly afterwards, the Central Bank of the People's Republic of China also cut interest rates. On October 8, 2008, there were sharp losses on stock markets worldwide with a loss of over 9% in Japan. Trading was suspended in Russia and Indonesia after steep morning losses. In the United States, following the funds cut by the Federal Reserve, stocks were volatile, finishing down. On October 8, 2008, the Federal Reserve loaned AIG $ 37.8 billion, in addition to the previous loan of $ 85 billion. The Central Bank of Iceland abandoned its attempt to peg the Icelandic Króna at 131 Króna/Euro after trying to set this peg on Monday, October 6, 2008. By Thursday October 9, 2008, the Icelandic Króna was trading at 340 to the euro when the government suspended all trade in the currency.

On Thursday, October 9, the Icelandic Financial Supervisory Authority took control of the country's biggest bank KaupÞing banki hf. This occurred when the Kaupthing Board resigned and asked the national authorities to take control. This came about when Britain transferred control of the business of Kaupthing Edge, its Internet bank, to ING Direct and put Kaupthing's UK operations into administration placing Kaupthing in technical default according to loan agreements. This marked an escalating row between Iceland and the United Kingdom over the growing crisis. All trade was also suspended on the Iceland Stock Exchange until Monday October 13, 2008.

On Thursday, October 9, 2008, the one-year anniversary of the Dow's peak, the cost of short term credit rose while there were heavy losses in the United States stock market. On this date, the Dow dropped below 8600, reaching a five year low. It was the first time since August 2003 that the Dow closed below 9000. Losses were moderate in Europe. The following day, Friday, October 10, 2008, there were large losses in Asian and European markets. Yamato Life filed for bankruptcy. Beset by falling commodities prices, Russia's stock markets remained closed on October 10. The Russian Parliament passed a plan authorizing lending of $ 36 billion gained from global oil sales to banks which met creditworthiness requirements. Special attention is being paid to shoring up Rosselkhozbank, the bank which provides credit to the reviving agricultural sector. The amount of funds available is limited due to falling oil prices. The government of the United States, as authorized by the Emergency Economic Stabilization Act, 2008, announced plans to infuse funds into banks by purchasing equity interests in them, in effect, partial nationalization, as done in Britain. The Treasury secretary Henry M. Paulson Jr. met Friday in Washington with world financial leaders. A meeting of international financial leaders hosted by President Bush at the White House in Washington is planned on Saturday to attempt to coordinate global response to the financial crisis.

On Friday, October 10th, stock markets crashed across Europe and Asia. London, Paris and Frankfurt dropped 10% within an hour of trading and again when Wall Street opened for trading. Global markets have experienced their worst weeks since 1987. Some indices like S and P 500 have seen the low since the Wall Street crash of 1929. Within the first five minutes of the trading session on Wall Street, the Dow Jones Industrial Average (DJIA) plunged 697 points, falling below 7900 to its lowest level since March 17, 2003. Later in the afternoon, the DJIA made violent swings back and forth across the breakeven line, toppling as much as 600 points and rising 322 points. The DJIA ended the day losing only 128 points, or 1.49%. Trading on New York Stock Exchange closed for the week with the Dow at 8,451, down 1,874 points, or 18% for the week, and after 8 days of losses, 40% down from its record high October 9, 2007. Trading on Friday was marked by extreme volatility with a steep loss in the first few minutes followed by a rise into positive territory, closing down at the end of the day. In S and P 100, some financial corporate showing signals upwards also. President George W. Bush reassured investors that the government will solve the financial crisis gripping world economies. The bonds of the bankrupt Lehman Brothers were also auctioned on Friday, October 10, 2008. They sold for a little over 8 cents.

As meetings proceeded with global financial leaders in Washington on Saturday, October 11, 2008, the United States government announced a change in emphasis in its rescue efforts from buying illiquid assets to recapitalizing banks, including strong banks, in exchange for preferred equity; and purchase of mortgages by Fannie Mae and Freddie Mac. These remedies were expected to be put into effect quicker than the prior plan which was estimated to take a month to set into operation.

Week of October 12, 2008

On Sunday, the British government was in negotiations with Royal Bank of Scotland, HBOS, Lloyds TSB and Barclays, major British banks, regarding recapitalization which would give the British government a substantial equity interest. An investment of more than 37 billion pounds is contemplated. Some purchases would be common stock with existing shareholders given a right of first refusal (the government would only purchase the shares if existing shareholders did not). Previously announced recapitalization plans contemplated only purchases of preferred equity without government participation in governance of the banks, however, as the financial emergency has rapidly developed, more aggressive measures are being advanced. On Sunday, October 12, 2008, European leaders, meeting in Paris, led by France and Germany, announced recapitalization plans for Europe's banks. Plans were announced to guarantee bank deposits for five years. European countries would finance their own rescue plans and tailor them to local conditions. Mechanisms are also planned to increase the availability of short-term credit. The total rescue plan totaled €1 trillion. Australia and New Zealand also announced bank guarantee plans. On Monday, October 13, 2008, the markets were closed in Japan and the bond market was closed in the United States.

On Sunday, in Norway, which is not in the euro zone, the Norwegian cabinet in a hastily called press conference announced a US $ 57.4 billion (350 billion Norwegian kroner) plan of offering Norwegian banks new government bonds.

The G7 nations, at their meeting in Washington over the weekend pledged to "support systemically important financial institutions and prevent their failure". This decision is based on analysis of the consequences of the bankruptcy of Lehman Brothers which resulted in the loss of funds by other financial institutions. It is thought that those losses may have triggered a tightening of the credit crunch as banks ceased to lend to one another. No enforceable mechanism was created to support the pledge, but it is believed to extend to major firms such as Morgan Stanley and Goldman Sachs.

On October 13, 2008, stock markets worldwide rose with the DJIA showing a 400 point leap at the start of trading. At the close of trading the average was up 936 points, a record climb, up 11%, closing above 9,000 at 9,387. After announcement in France of a 320 billion euro rescue and guarantee plan, French CAC40 rose by 11.18% within the day. Germany announced a €400 billion plan. On Monday the International Monetary Fund offered possible technical and financial aid to Hungary which has suffered during the crisis due to the flight of investors to euro, Swiss franc, and dollar denominated investments. As in the rest of the world, on Monday stock prices rose on the Hungarian exchange and pressure on the national currency, the Forint eased. The Forint has dropped 30% against the dollar since July. The prime minister of Spain, Jose Luis Rodriguez Zapatero, announced that Spain would provide up to €100 billion of guarantees for new debt issued by commercial banks in 2008. This plan followed a meeting at the Euro-zone summit over the weekend to try to develop a coordinated effort to combat the credit crisis. The UK government started the nationalization process by injecting £37 billion in the nation's three largest banks. The UK government would end up owning a majority share in the Royal Bank of Scotland (RBS) and over a 40% share in Lloyds and HBOS. In return for the bailout, the banks agreed to cancel dividend payments until the loans are repaid, have board members appointed by the Treasury, and limit executive pay. The European Central Bank attempted to revive credit market by weekly injections of unlimited euro funds at an interest rate of 3.75%. The ECB president, Jean-Claude Trichet, was also contemplating relaxing the collateral standards to make the funds more accessible to banks. Following its European partners, Italy pledged to intervene as necessary to prevent any bank failures in its country. Finance Minister, Giulio Tremonti, said Italy would guarantee new bank bonds of up to 5 years until the end of 2009 and the Bank of Italy would provide € 40 billion in treasury bills to banks to refinance inferior assets that can not be currently used as collateral. In coordination with other Euro-zone countries, the Dutch government announced that it would guarantee inter bank lending up to € 200 billion. This followed the set-up of a € 20 billion Dutch fund to help recapitalize banks and insurers.

On Tuesday the United States announced a plan to take an equity interest of $ 250 billion in US banks with 25 billion going to each of the four largest banks. The 9 largest banks in the US: Goldman Sachs, Morgan Stanley, J.P. Morgan, Bank of America, Merrill Lynch, Citigroup, Wells Fargo, Bank of New York Mellon and State Street were called in to a meeting on Monday morning and pressured to sign; all eventually agreed. The plan will be open to any bank for 30 days. The equity interests purchased by the government are preferred shares that pay 5% but rise to 9% after 5 years; it is expected that the companies will repurchase this interest when they can raise private capital to do so. The plan also includes an option allowing the government to purchase common stock according to a formula which could return substantial profit to the taxpayers should the stock price of the companies substantially appreciate. The total liability assumed is $ 2.25 trillion including a $ 1.5 trillion guarantee of new senior debt issued by banks and a $ 500 billion guarantee of deposits in non-interest-bearing accounts.

Also on that day, United Arab Emirates' (UAE) Ministry of Finance added a $ 19 billion liquidity injection to domestic banks bringing the total dollars injected to $ 32.7 billion. The UAE central bank offered 13.6 billion in liquidity to help domestic banks in September. To protect local deposits, the UAE government guaranteed all deposits and inter-bank lending. Japan announced a plan that will help steady the Japanese market and avoid the worse of the credit crisis. Among the measures included are lifting restrictions on companies buying back their shares, strengthening disclosure on short selling, and the temporary suspension of the sale of government-owned stocks. The Australian government unveiled a $ 10.4 billion stimulus package. The Economic Security Strategy is designed to help pensioners, low and middle income families, and first time home buyers withstand the credit crisis and global economic slowdown. This followed the Australian government announcing that it would guarantee all bank deposits for three years, guarantee all term wholesaling funding by Australian banks in international markets and double its planned purchase of residential mortgage backed securities. The Icelandic stock exchange began trading again after a three day shutdown.

On Wednesday, October 15, all the European, American and Asian major stock exchanges collapsed upto 9 per cent. On October 16, a rescue plan was announced for the Swiss banks UBS and Credit Suisse. Recapitalization involved Swiss government funds, private investors, and the sovereign wealth fund of Qatar. A Swiss agency was set-up to purchase and workout toxic funds. UBS had suffered substantial withdrawals by domestic Swiss depositors but still reported profits; Credit Suisse has reported losses. Most large banks in the United States continued to report large losses.

Week of October 19, 2008

Following a conference at Camp David over the weekend of October 18th and 19th of 2008, attended by President Nicolas Sarkozy of France and José Manuel Barroso, President of the European Commission, President George W. Bush announced on Wednesday, October 22 that he would host an international conference of financial leaders on November 15 in Washington, D.C. Participants would be drawn from both the developed world and the developing world, including participants from the G20 industrial nations such as India, Brazil and China.

On Sunday, October 19, 2008, the government of the Netherlands bailed out ING, the Dutch bank, with a € 10 billion capital rescue plan. On Monday the government of Belgium rescued the insurance company Ethias with a € 1.5 billion capital injection. In Germany BayernLB has decided to apply for funds from the German € 500 billion rescue program. Sweden announced formation of a 1.5 trillion kronor fund to support inter-bank lending and a 15 billion kronor capital injection plan. Swedish banks were reported to be increasingly affected by the financial crisis. An IMF rescue plan for Iceland was reported to be near finalization while Ukraine was reported to be in discussions with the IMF. Iceland was reported to have also received assistance from Denmark and Norway while Britain has offered a loan to support compensation of British depositors in failed Icelandic bank Landsbanki. On Monday France announced a € 10.5 billion rescue plan for six of its largest banks, including Crédit Agricole, BNP and Société Générale.

Despite some improvement in the availability of credit, stock markets and weak currencies such as the British pound and the euro continued to decline worldwide during the week of October 19. Markets across Asia suffered particularly heavy losses while European markets experienced substantial losses too, but to a lesser extent compared to those in Asia. The Dow Industrials Index, on the other hand, experienced a week of extreme volatility with violent swings upwards and downwards, eventually ending lower. The yen and the dollar showed particular strength with the yen rising with respect to the dollar. This "flight to quality" had baleful effects on the economies of all nations including the United States and Japan. On Wednesday, Pakistan joined Iceland, Hungary, Serbia and Ukraine and requested aid from the International Monetary Fund in dealing with severe balance of payments difficulties. Hungary, Russia, Ukraine, Pakistan, Turkey, South Africa, Argentina, Iceland, Estonia, Latvia, Lithuania, Romania and Bulgaria were all experiencing financial difficulties with others threatened. These countries did not hold securities based on subprime mortgages, but were affected by inability to borrow money, the credit crisis.

On Friday, October 24, 2008, stock markets plummeted worldwide amidst growing fears among investors that a deep global recession is imminent if not already settled in. The panic was partly fueled by remarks made by Alan Greenspan that the crisis is "a once-in-a-century credit tsunami" and by comments made by Gordon Brown during a speech, admitting essentially that Great Britain is already in recession mode. Following the trend, the US stock markets also fell sharply on opening and ended with the Dow Industrial Index down 312 points. Friday and Saturday (October 24 and 25) the 7th Asia-Europe Meeting was held in Beijing with the European Union meeting Asian states in an attempt to discuss a common approach ahead of the Emergency International Meeting that is scheduled to take place in Washington on November 15. No specific recommendations to solve the crisis were developed.

Week of October 26, 2008

On Sunday, October 26, 2008, Hungary and Ukraine made tentative arrangements with the International Monetary Fund for emergency aid packages. In Poland the value of stocks has fallen 50% for the year and the zloty, the Polish currency, has fallen against both the dollar and the euro. The crisis has affected South Africa, Brazil and Turkey. South Africa was particularly affected by a dramatic drop in the price of platinum, a commodity used in automobile manufacturing. In the Gulf States, impacted by the falling price of oil and a drop in equities prices of 40% for the year, the Gulf Cooperation Council met in Riyadh on Saturday to discuss a coordinated response to the crisis.

On Monday, October 27, 2008, Hong Kong stocks crashed, losing more than 12% of their value while in Japan, the Nikkei 225 Index plummeted by 6.4% to its lowest level since 1982. European stock markets showed mixed results. After suffering an initial drop, the Dow Jones Industrial Average was in slightly positive territory for much of the trading day but eventually closed down 203 points. Oil futures continued to decline and the yen continued to rise against all other currencies. There was consideration given by both the G7 and the Japanese government to take measures to support other currencies as against the yen.

In a second round of recapitalization, the U.S. Treasury funded 22 banks with 38 billion dollars. Criteria for funding were based on the strength of the bank with stronger banks with higher CAMELS ratings having a greater chance of being offered aid. The American Bankers Association stated that due to restrictions on salaries and payment of dividends that some U.S. banks may not participate. Another concern was that acceptance of the recapitalization plan might give a false signal that a bank was troubled.

On Tuesday, October 28, stocks rose dramatically worldwide in anticipation of rate cuts by central banks. In the U.S. the Dow Industrial Average rose 10.8%, closing at over 9000. On Wednesday, October 29, markets in the U.S. closed down slightly despite announcement by the Federal Open Market Committee of a reduction in the federal funds rate 50 points to 1 percent. Markets in the U.S. were up Thursday and

Friday, closing up for the week, cutting losses to the Dow Industrial Average during October to 17%, down 30% for the year.

In Russia, the $ 50 billion rescue program administered by the state development bank Vnesheconombank (VEB) is assisting Russian firms controlled by Russian oligarchs who gave ownership of portions of their companies as security for loans from Western financial institutions. Stock markets in Russian have crashed, down 70% and there is lack of faith in its currency the ruble. Despite significant foreign reserves from the sale of oil, Russia is now faced with sharply reduced commodities prices.

In Asia, Japan announced its second economic stimulus plan of $ 51 billion on Thursday, October 30. Hong Kong and Taiwan cut interest rates, while an interest cut of 0.3% was announced by the Bank of Japan on Friday. Also on Thursday the Federal Reserve established a $ 30 billion currency swap line with South Korea and Singapore as well as Brazil and Mexico.

JPMorgan Chase, the largest bank in the United States, announced that it would work with homeowners who demonstrate a willingness to pay their mortgages by reducing interest payments or principal. Counseling centers are planned for troubled areas. Washington Mutual, and EMC Mortgage Corporation, a loan servicing company, acquired by J.P. Morgan, will be included. Bank of America has announced a similar program, as has Countrywide Financial as the result of a court settlement.

THE MONTH OF NOVEMBER, 2008

Week of November 2, 2008

Reports of Economic Activity

October sales of cars and light trucks in the United States fell precipitously in 2008 when compared with sales in October 2007, with General Motors falling 45%, Ford falling 30%, Chrysler falling 35%, Toyota falling 23%, Honda falling 25%, and Nissan falling 33%. Much of the falloff in sales was attributable to customers being unable to arrange financing.

Except for Wal-Mart, which posted a slight gain, retail sales were off during October 2008 as compared with October 2007 in the United States with some moderate priced stores reporting double digit decreases. October retail sales were down 4.1% from October 2007 and down 2.8% from September 2008. In the UK car sales fell by 23% in October, following a 21% decline in September.

Employment reports released by the Labor Department on Friday, November 7, showed that about 500,000 jobs were lost in the United States during September and October 2008 with unemployment rising to 6.5% at the end of October. It is anticipated by experts that unemployment will rise to 8% by the middle of 2009.

Events

Amid predictions of a "deep recession" in the UK and the Euro-zone, on Thursday, November 6, the Bank of England, citing a reduced danger of inflation due to falling commodities prices, lowered its base rate by 1.5 percentage points, from 4.5% to 3%. This was accompanied by a 50 basis point drop in the base rate to 3.25% by the European Central Bank (ECB). The IMF at Washington D.C, predicted for 2009 a word wide 0.3% decrease of the BIP for the developed economies.

Week of November 9, 2008

George, W. Bush addressing a Manhattan Institute-sponsored event at Federal Hall on November 13, 2008, speaking against too much government involvement in resolving the crisis. On Sunday, November 9, the People's Republic of China announced a $ 586 billion domestic stimulus package for the remainder of 2008, 2009, and 2010. Economic growth has slowed in China with sharp drops in property and stock values. The money from the stimulus package will be spent on upgrading infrastructure, particularly roads, railways, airports and the power grids throughout the country and raise rural incomes via land reform. Also spending will be made on social welfare projects such as affordable housing and environmental protection. Some Chinese factories engaged in low-end export manufacturing have gone out of business.

On Monday, November 10, the US Treasury announced investment of 40 billion dollars in preferred stock of AIG, adjusting the terms of the existing credit line and its amount. Total exposure, including equity and debt, is now 150 billion dollars. Funds were drawn from the Troubled Asset Relief Program which was not available at the time of the original bailout of AIG. The question of whether emergency funding would be made available to the troubled American auto industry remained under consideration.

On November 12, US Treasury Secretary Henry Paulson scrapped the original Troubled Asset Relief Program (TARP) and announced shift in the focus to consumer lending. The remaining portion of the TARP budget will be used to help relieve pressure on consumer credits such as car loans, student loans, credit cards, etc.

On Thursday November 13, the Dow Jones Industrial Average marked another dramatic session, with the index (opening at 8,282.66) that after a mixed start tumbled again below the 8,000 mark (to a low of 7,965.42) but then reversed the trend and gained more than 900 points (fourth largest daily swing ever) in less than three hours closing at 8,835.25 with a net gain of more than 550 points (third largest ever).

The prospect of a federal bailout of failing US automakers appeared dim pending the inauguration of Barack Obama. There appeared to be opposition from both the Republican members of the Senate and the office of the incumbent president, George W. Bush, which expressed doubt that the companies could be salvaged.

At the invitation of US President George W. Bush the leaders of the G-20 held the initial session of the Summit on Financial Markets and the World Economy on Saturday, November 15, in Washington, D.C. They agreed to cooperate with respect to the global financial crisis and issued a statement regarding immediate and medium term goals and actions considered necessary to support and reform the international economy. The initial session, attended by the leaders of the G-20 set forth a road map of proposed reforms which will be followed up in coming months by the development of specific proposals, including a comprehensive reform of the Bretton Woods Institutions.

Week of November 16, 2008

Reports of Economic Activity

In the third quarter of 2008 the gross domestic product of Japan fell 0.4% following a 3.7% drop in the second quarter. Similar reports of recession level economic activity had been released previously by Hong Kong, Germany and the European Union. It was widely anticipated that economic activity in the United States would be found to be at recession levels when statistics were released. As of November 20 new applications for unemployment benefits rose to a seasonally adjusted 542,000 per week; new applications averaged over 500,000 a week for the last four weeks.

Events

On Wednesday, November 19, proposed federal bailouts of US auto makers failed with Republican senators rejecting the Democratic plan and Democratic senators rejecting the Republican plan. Negotiations continued with the Democrats requesting a plan for viability from the automakers. Automobile sales were also down sharply in Europe and bailouts were under consideration, particularly for subsidiaries of General Motors and Vauxhall in the United Kingdom.

On Wednesday, November 19 and 20, the stock indices of all over the globe fell drastically on an average of over 5%. The biggest fall was in financial sector shares.

On Friday, November 21 the Dow Jones Industrial Average recovered about half of the loss for the week and closed above 8,000; however, stocks of Citibank, Bank of America, and J.P. Morgan Chase continued to decline. It was unclear whether the drop in the value of Citigroup stock to under $ 4 reflected financial weakness of the bank or what rescue plan could be crafted. One theory for the disappointment of investors was that the failure of the Treasury to purchase toxic mortgage related securities held by the bank left billions of unrealized losses on the books. Citigroup continues to hold $ 20 billion in mortgage-related securities, currently valued at a substantial discount.

As of the week of November 16 stock losses in United States markets during 2008 as measured by the S and P 500 were equivalent to those suffered in 1931, over 50%. Total losses during the Great Depression exceeded 80% but that was over a three year period.

Week of November 23, 2008

Late on Sunday, November 23, a rescue plan for Citigroup was agreed by the United States government. In a joint statement by the Treasury Department, the Federal Reserve and the Federal Deposit Insurance Corp it was announced that in exchange for preferred stock valued at $ 27 billion paying 8% interest, a further $ 20 billion would be invested into the company and that the government would limit loss on $ 306 billion in risky loans and securities to 29 billion dollars plus 10% of any remaining losses.

Friday, November 21 and Monday, November 24 marked the Dow Jones Industrial Average's largest two-session gain since October 1987. The Dow gained 891.10 points, 11.8%, bringing it to a close at 8,443.39 points.

THE MONTH OF DECEMBER, 2008

Week of December 1, 2008

Reports of Economic Activity

On December 1, the National Bureau of Economic Research officially declared that the U.S. economy had entered recession in December, 2007. The Labor Department said that the US lost 533,000 jobs in November 2008, the biggest monthly loss since 1974. This raised the unemployment rate from 6.5% to 6.7%.

Events in the Week of December 1

After 5 positive days the previous week, all the major stock indices of USA fell heavily. Oil fell below $ 50 a barrel in New York Trading. The General Accounting Office released a report that claims that the Oversight of the Troubled Assets Relief Program requires additional actions to ensure "integrity, accountability, and transparency".

Week of December 8, 2008

Reports of Economic Activity

On December 9, the Bank of Canada lowered its key interest rate by 0.75% to 1.5%, the lowest it had been since 1958; at the same time the Bank officially announced that Canada's economy was in recession. This move came after the news that Canada lost 70,600 jobs in the month of November, the most since 1982. On December 11, the FBI announces the arrest of Bernard Madoff in a Ponzi scheme which totals $ 50 billion by Madoff's own estimate, and which is soon found to affect banks, individuals, and charities in the U.S. and Europe.

Week of December 22, 2008

This week is cut short by the Christmas holiday. US industry leaders ask the Federal Reserve for assistance unfreezing the commercial real estate market, which has not securitized any loans in the last six months of 2008.

THE MONTH OF JANUARY, 2009

The global financial crisis continues in the year 2009 too with the failure of some more financial institutions and the government of different countries continues to try with several measures to come out of the crisis. On the evening of 18 January, 2009, the Danish Parliament, agreed to a financial package worth 100 billion Danish Krone (17.6 billion USD). On January 22, the editorial board of *The Christian Science Monitor* wrote that the four largest U.S. banks "have lost half of their value since January 2."

Global Responses to the Crisis

Responses in Asia/Pacific

On September 15, 2008 China cut its interest rate for the first time since 2002. Indonesia reduced its overnight repo rate by two percentage points to 10.25 percent. The Reserve Bank of Australia injected nearly $ 1.5 billion into the banking system, nearly three times as much as the market's estimated requirement. The Reserve Bank of India added almost $ 1.32 billion, through a refinance operation, its biggest in at least a month. On November 9, 2008 the Chinese economic stimulus plan is a RMB¥ 4 trillion ($ 586 billion) stimulus package announced by the central government of the People's Republic of China in its biggest move to stop the global financial crisis from hitting the world's fourth largest economy. A statement on the government's website said the State Council had approved a plan to invest 4 trillion Yuan ($ 586 billion) in infrastructure and social welfare by the end of 2010. The stimulus package will be invested in key areas such as housing, rural infrastructure, transportation, health and education, environment, industry, disaster rebuilding, income-building, tax cuts, and finance. China's export driven economy is starting to feel the impact of the economic slowdown in the United States and Europe, and the government has already cut key interest rates three times in less than two months in a bid to spur economic expansion. On the 28th of November, China Ministry of Finance and the State Administration of Taxation jointly announced a rise in export tax rebate rates on some labor-intensive goods. The stimulus package was welcomed by world leaders and analysts as larger than expected and a sign that by boosting its own economy, China is helping to stabilize the global economy. However, Marc Faber January 16th said that China according to him was in recession.

In Taiwan, the central bank on September 16, 2008 said it would cut its required reserve ratios for the first time in eight years. The central bank added $ 3.59 billion into the foreign-currency inter bank market the same day. Bank of Japan pumped $ 29.3 billion into the financial system on September 17, 2008 and the Reserve Bank of Australia added $ 3.45 billion the same day.

U.S. Responses

The Federal Reserve, Treasury, and SEC took several steps on September 19, 2008, to intervene in the crisis. To stop the potential run on money market mutual funds, the Treasury also announced on September 19 a new $ 50 billion program to insure the investments, similar to the Federal Deposit Insurance Corporation (FDIC) program. Part of the announcements included temporary exceptions to section 23A and 23B (Regulation W), allowing financial groups to more easily share funds within their group. The exceptions would expire on January 30, 2009, unless extended by the Federal Reserve Board. The Securities and Exchange Commission announced termination of short-selling of 799 financial stocks, as well as action against naked short selling.

During the week ending September 19, 2008, money market mutual funds had begun to experience significant withdrawals of funds by investors. This created a significant risk because money market funds are integral to the ongoing financing of corporations of all types. Individual investors lend money to money market funds, which then provide the funds to corporations in exchange for corporate short-term securities called asset-backed commercial paper (ABCP). However, a potential bank run had begun on certain money market funds. If this situation had worsened, the ability of major corporations to secure needed short-term financing through ABCP issuance would have been significantly affected. To assist with liquidity throughout the system, the Treasury and Federal Reserve Bank announced that banks could obtain funds via the Federal Reserve's Discount Window using ABCP as collateral.

The Federal Reserve of the USA has cut the interest rate over the period of time from January 2008 to October 2008. The interest rate as on October 2008 was reduced to 0.5%.

The Secretary of the United States Treasury, Henry Paulson and President George W. Bush proposed legislation for the government to purchase up to US $ 700 billion of "troubled mortgage-related assets" from financial firms in hopes of improving confidence in the mortgage-backed securities markets and the financial firms participating in it. Discussion, hearings and meetings among legislative leaders and the administration later made clear that the proposal would undergo significant change before it could be approved by Congress. On October 1, a revised compromise version was approved by the Senate with a 74-25 vote.

In an effort to increase available funds for commercial banks and lower the fed funds rate, on September 29 the U.S. Federal Reserve announced plans to double its Term Auction

Facility to $ 300 billion. Because there appeared to be a shortage of U.S. dollars in Europe at that time, the Federal Reserve also announced it would increase its swap facilities with foreign central banks from $ 290 billion to $ 620 billion. As of December 24, 2008, the Federal Reserve had used its independent authority to spend $ 1.2 trillion on purchasing various financial assets and making emergency loans to address the financial crisis, above and beyond the $ 700 billion authorized by Congress from the federal budget. This includes emergency loans to banks, credit card companies, and general businesses, temporary swaps of treasury bills for mortgage-backed securities, the sale of Bear Stearns, and the bailouts of American International Group (AIG), Fannie Mae and Freddie Mac, and Citigroup.

Responses in the European Union

The European Central Bank injected $ 99.8 billion in a one-day money-market auction. The Bank of England pumped in $ 36 billion. Altogether, central banks throughout the world added more than $ 200 billion from the beginning of the week to September 17. On September 29, 2008 the Belgian, Luxembourg and Dutch authorities partially nationalized Fortis. The German government bailed out Hypo Real Estate. On 8 October 2008 the British Government announced a bank rescue package of around £ 500 billion ($ 850 billion at the time). The plan comprises three parts. First, £ 200 billion will be made available to the banks in the Bank of England's Special Liquidity scheme. Second, the Government will increase the banks' market capitalisation, through the Bank Recapitalization Fund, with an initial £ 25 billion and another £ 25 billion to be provided if needed. Third, the Government will temporarily underwrite any eligible lending between British banks up to around £ 250 billion. In early December German Finance Minister Peer Steinbrück indicated that he does not believe in a "Great Rescue Plan" and indicated reluctance to spend more money addressing the crisis.

CONCLUSION

The global financial crisis of 2008-09 is the recent financial crisis amongst all the financial crises of the world. The crisis was started in USA and gradually it has taken the whole world in its grip as the economy of all the countries are somehow related to the USA economy. The governments of different countries are still fighting with this crisis and only time will say when this crisis is going to be end.

Sub-Prime Mortgage Crisis

The *sub-prime mortgage crisis* is the recent financial crisis. It is triggered by a dramatic rise in mortgage delinquencies and foreclosures in the United States, with major adverse consequences for banks and financial markets around the globe. The crisis, which has its roots in the closing years of the 20th century, became apparent in 2007 and has exposed pervasive weaknesses in financial industry regulation and the global financial system.

Overview of the Chapter

The current ongoing sub-prime crisis is basically due to the burst of the US housing bubble. The chapter discusses the crisis in detail. The contents of the chapter are given as follows:

- Background of the Crisis
- Causes of the Crisis
- Impact of Crisis
- Responses to the Crisis
- Effect on Financial Condition of US Govt. Units
- Depression
- Conclusion

Many USA mortgages issued in recent years were made to sub-prime borrowers. The sub-prime borrowers are defined as those with lesser ability to repay the loan based on various criteria. When USA house prices began to decline in 2006-07, mortgage delinquencies soared, and securities backed with sub-prime mortgages, widely held by financial firms, lost most of their value. The result has been a large decline in the capital of many banks and USA government sponsored enterprises, tightening credit around the world.

BACKGROUND OF THE CRISIS

The crisis began with the bursting of the United States housing bubble and high default rates on "sub-prime" and adjustable rate mortgages (ARM), beginning in approximately 2005-06. Government policies and competitive pressures for several years prior to the crisis encouraged higher risk lending practices. Further, an increase in loan incentives such as easy initial terms and a long-term trend of rising housing prices had encouraged borrowers to assume difficult mortgages in the belief they would be able to quickly refinance at more favourable terms. However, once interest rates began to rise and housing prices started to drop moderately in 2006-07 in many parts of the U.S., refinancing became more difficult. Defaults and foreclosure activity increased dramatically as easy initial terms expired, home prices failed to go up as anticipated, and ARM interest rates reset higher. Foreclosures accelerated in the United States in late 2006 and triggered a global financial crisis through 2007 and 2008. During 2007, nearly 1.3 million U.S. housing properties were subject to foreclosure activity, up 79% from 2006.

The mortgage-backed securities (MBS), which derive their value from mortgage payments and housing prices, had enabled financial institutions and investors around the world to invest in the U.S. housing market. Major Banks and financial institutions had borrowed and invested heavily in MBS and reported losses of approximately US $ 435 billion as of 17 July 2008. The key financial institutions became concerned of the liquidity and solvency. It drove central banks to take necessary action to encourage lending by the banks to the worthy borrowers. It was done by providing funds to the banks by the central banks. It also helped in restoring faith in the commercial paper markets, which are integral to funding business operations. During that time governments also bailed out certain key financial institutions. As a result of these governments have to assume significant additional financial commitments.

Almost all the major central banks of different countries have cut the interest rates to help the governments to come out of the crisis and implement economic stimulus package. To restore confidence in the financial market was also one of the major reasons for these actions. The restoring confidence in the market was one of the major challenges because between January 1 and October 11, 2008 investors have lost around $ 8 Trillion in USA alone. In November, 2008 the leaders from the larger developed and emerging nations met to formulate strategies for addressing the crisis.

Mortgage Market

In the root of the sub-prime crisis was the practice of lending mainly in the form of mortgages for the purchase of residences to borrowers who do not fulfil the required criteria for borrowing at the lowest prevailing market interest rate. Borrower's credit score, credit history and other factors are considered while framing these criteria. In this case if a borrower is not in making timely mortgage payments to the loan servicer, the lender can take possession of the residence acquired using the proceeds from the mortgage, which is technically called foreclosure.

As on March 2007, the value of USA sub-prime mortgages was estimated at $ 1.3 trillion. There are over 7.5 million first-lien subprime mortgages outstanding. During 2004-06, the share of subprime mortgages relative to total originations ranged from 18%-21%, versus less than 10% in 2001-03. In the third quarter of 2007, there were 43% accounted foreclosures. It is an increase of 79% over 2006. This figure in 2008 has increased by 81% over 2007. By October 2007, approximately 16% of sub-prime adjustable rate mortgages (ARM) were either 90-days delinquent or the lender had begun foreclosure proceedings, which is three times the rate of 2005. By January 2008, the delinquency rate had risen to 21% and by May 2008 it was 25%. Between August 2007 and October 2008, 936,439 USA residences completed foreclosure.

The Growth of the Bubble

Over the past 60 years, a variety of financial innovations have gradually made it possible for lenders to sell the right to receive the payments on the mortgages they issue, through a process called securitization. The resulting securities are called mortgage backed securities (MBS) and collateralized debt obligations (CDO). Most American mortgages are now held by mortgage pools, the generic term for MBS and CDOs. Of the $ 10.6 trillion of USA residential mortgages outstanding as of mid year 2008, $ 6.6 trillion were held by mortgage pools and $ 3.4 trillion by traditional depository institutions.

This "originate to distribute" model means that investors holding MBS and CDOs also bear several types of risks, and this has a variety of consequences. There are four primary types of risk.

Name	*Description*
Credit risk	The risk that the homeowner or borrower will be unable or unwilling to pay back the loan.
Asset price risk	The risk that assets (MBS in this case) will depreciate in value, resulting in financial losses, markdowns and possibly margin calls.
Liquidity risk	The risk that a business entity will be unable to obtain financing, such as from the commercial paper market.
Counterparty risk	The risk that a party to a contract will be unable or unwilling to uphold their obligations.
	The aggregate effect of these and other risks has recently been called systemic risk, which refers to when formerly uncorrelated risks shift and become highly correlated, damaging the entire financial system.

When homeowners default, the payments received by MBS and CDO investors decline and the perceived credit risk rises. This has had a significant adverse effect on investors and the entire mortgage industry. The effect is magnified by the high debt levels households and businesses have incurred in recent years. Finally, the risks associated with American mortgage lending have global impacts because of the integration of the USA economy with the world economy in a closer way.

There was an option to the investors in MBS and CDOs to insure against credit risk by buying credit defaults swaps (CDS). As mortgage defaults rose, the likelihood that the issuers of CDS would have to pay their counterparties increased amount. This created uncertainty across the system, as investors wondered if CDS issuers would honour their commitments.

CAUSES OF THE CRISIS

There are a number of factors which are pervasive in both housing and credit markets. Some of the factors are like the inability of homeowners to make their mortgage payments, poor judgment by borrowers and/or lenders, speculation and overbuilding during the boom period, risky mortgage products, high personal and corporate debt levels, financial products that distributed and perhaps concealed the risk of mortgage default, monetary policy, international trade imbalances, and government regulation. Ultimately, though, moral hazard lay at the core of many of the causes. In its "Declaration of the Summit on Financial Markets and the World Economy," dated 15 November 2008, leaders of the Group of 20 cited the following causes:

"During a period of strong global growth, growing capital flows, and prolonged stability earlier this decade, market participants sought higher yields without an adequate appreciation of the risks and failed to exercise proper due diligence. At the same time, weak underwriting standards, unsound risk management practices, increasingly complex and opaque financial products, and consequent excessive leverage combined to create vulnerabilities in the system. Policy-makers, regulators and supervisors, in some advanced countries, did not adequately appreciate and address the risks building up in financial markets, keep pace with financial innovation, or take into account the systemic ramifications of domestic regulatory actions."

Boom and Bust in the Housing Market

Prior to the crisis, low interest rates and large inflows of foreign funds have created easy credit conditions for a number of years. It has fueled the housing market boom and encouraged debt-financed consumption. In USA, the rate of home owners has increased from 64% in 1994 (about where it had been since 1980) to an all-time high of 69.2% in 2004. This increase in the home ownership rate and demand for the housing was made possible due to the subprime lending. It has driven the price higher. Between 1997 and 2006, the price of the American house increased by 124%. During the two decades ending in 2001, the national median home price ranged from 2.9 to 3.1 times median household income. This ratio rose to 4.0 in 2004 and 4.6 in 2006. This housing bubble resulted in quite a few homeowners refinancing their homes at lower interest rates, or financing consumer spending by taking out second mortgages secured by the price appreciation. USA household debt as a percentage of annual disposable personal income was 127% at the end of 2007, versus 77% in 1990.

While there was an increase in the housing prices, consumers were saving less and both borrowing and spending by the consumers shows an increasing trend. Starting in 2005, American households have spent more than 99.5% of their disposable personal income on consumption or interest payments. If imputations mostly pertaining to owner-occupied housing are removed from these calculations, American households have spent more than their disposable personal income in every year starting in 1999. Household debt grew from $ 705 billion at year-end 1974 which was 60% of disposable personal income, to $ 7.4 trillion at yearend 2000, and finally to $ 14.5 trillion in midyear 2008, 134% of disposable personal income. During 2008, the typical USA household owned 13 credit cards.

This credit and house price explosion led to a building boom and eventually to a surplus of unsold homes, which caused U.S. housing prices to peak and begin declining in mid-2006. Easy credit, and a belief that house prices would continue to appreciate, had encouraged many subprime borrowers to obtain adjustable-rate mortgages. These mortgages enticed borrowers with a below market interest rate for some predetermined period, followed by market interest rates for the remainder of the mortgage's term. Borrowers who could not make the higher payments once the initial grace period ended would try to refinance their mortgages. Refinancing became more difficult, once house prices began to decline in many parts of the USA. Borrowers who found themselves unable to escape higher monthly payments by refinancing began to default.

As more borrowers stop paying their mortgage payments, foreclosures and the supply of homes for sale increase. This places downward pressure on housing prices, which further lowers homeowners' equity. The decline in mortgage payments also reduces the value of mortgage-backed securities, which erodes the net worth and financial health of banks. This vicious cycle is at the heart of the crisis.

By September 2008, average U.S. housing prices had declined by over 20% from their mid-2006 peak. This major and unexpected decline in house prices means that many borrowers have zero or negative equity in their homes, meaning their homes were worth less than their mortgages. As of March 2008, an estimated 8.8 million borrowers—10.8% of all homeowners—had negative equity in their homes, a number that is believed to have risen to 12 million by November 2008. Borrowers in this situation have an incentive to "walk away" from their mortgages and abandon their homes, even though doing so will damage their credit rating for a number of years.

Increasing foreclosure rates increases the inventory of houses offered for sale. The number of new homes sold in 2007 was 26.4% less than in the preceding year. By January 2008, the inventory of unsold new homes was 9.8 times the December 2007 sales volume, the highest value of this ratio since 1981. Furthermore, nearly four million existing homes were for sale, of which almost 2.9 million were vacant. This overhang of unsold homes lowered house prices. As prices declined, more homeowners were at risk of default or foreclosure. House prices are expected to continue declining until this inventory of unsold homes (an instance of excess supply) declines to normal levels.

Speculation

Speculation in residential real estate has been a contributing factor. During 2006, 22% of homes purchased (1.65 million units) were for investment purposes, with an additional 14% (1.07 million units) purchased as vacation homes. During 2005, these figures were 28% and 12%, respectively. In other words, a record level of nearly 40% of homes purchases were not intended as primary residences. Housing prices nearly doubled between 2000 and 2006. While homes had not traditionally been treated as investments subject to speculation, this behavior changed during the housing boom.

Individuals investing in equities have margin (borrowing) restrictions and receive warnings regarding the risk to principal; there are no such requirements for home buyers. While stock brokers are prohibited from telling an investor that a stock or bond investment cannot lose money, it was not illegal for mortgage brokers to do so. Equity investors are well-aware of the need to diversify their financial holdings, but for many homeowners the home represented both a leveraged and concentrated risk. Further, in the U.S. capital gains on stocks are taxed more aggressively than housing appreciation, which has large exemptions. These factors all enabled speculative behaviour. Keynesian economist Hyman Minsky described three types of speculative borrowing that contribute to rising debt and an eventual collapse of asset values:

- The "hedge borrower," who expects to make debt payments from cash flows from other investments;
- The "speculative borrower," who borrows believing that he can service the interest on his loan, but who must continually roll over the principal into new investments; and
- The "Ponzi borrower," who relies on the appreciation of the value of his assets to refinance or pay-off his debt, while being unable to repay the original loan.

High-Risk Mortgage Loans and Lending/Borrowing Practices

Lenders began to offer more and more loans to higher-risk borrowers, including illegal immigrants. Subprime mortgages amounted to $ 35 billion (5% of total originations) in 1994, 9% in 1996, $ 160 billion (13%) in 1999, and $ 600 billion (20%) in 2006. A study by the Federal Reserve found that the average difference between subprime and prime mortgage interest rates (the "sub-prime markup") declined from 280 basis points in 2001, to 130 basis points in 2007. In other words, the risk premium required by lenders to offer a sub-prime loan declined. This occurred even though the credit ratings of sub-prime borrowers, and the characteristics of sub-prime loans, both declined during the 2001–06 period, which should have had the opposite effect. In addition to considering high-risk borrowers, lenders have offered increasingly risky loan options and borrowing incentives. In 2005, the median down payment for first-time home buyers was 2%, with 43% of those buyers making no down payment at all. One high-risk option was the "No Income, No Job and No Assets" loans, sometimes referred to as Ninja loans. Another example is the interest-only adjustable-rate mortgage (ARM), which allows the homeowner to pay just the interest (not principal) during an initial period.

Mortgage underwriting practices were criticized on the ground that these loans were not subjected to appropriate review and documentation. In 2007, 40% of all subprime loans resulted from automated underwriting. The mortgage brokers with the intention of profiting from the home loan did not thoroughly examine the repayment capacity of the borrowers. Hence the mortgage fraud by borrowers increased.

Securitization Practices

Securitization, a form of structured finance, involves the pooling of financial assets, especially those for which there is no ready secondary market, such as mortgages, credit card receivables, student loans. The pooled assets serve as collateral for new financial assets issued by the entity owning the underlying assets.

Securitization, combined with investor appetite for mortgage-backed securities (MBS), and the high ratings formerly granted to MBSs by rating agencies, meant that mortgages with a high risk of default could be originated almost at will, with the risk shifted from the mortgage issuer to investors at large. Securitization meant that issuers could repeatedly relend a given sum, greatly increasing their fee income. Since issuers no longer carried any default risk, they had every incentive to lower their underwriting standards to increase their loan volume and total profit.

With the advent of securitization, the traditional model has given way to the "originate to distribute" model, in which the credit risk is transferred (distributed) to investors through MBS and CDOs. Securitization created a secondary market for mortgages, and meant that those issuing mortgages were no longer required to hold them to maturity.

Securitization accelerated in the mid-1990s. The securitized share of subprime mortgages (i.e., those passed to third-party investors via MBS) increased from 54% in 2001, to 75% in 2006. The securitization markets started to close down in the spring of 2007 and nearly shut-down in the fall of 2008. More than a third of the private credit markets thus became unavailable as a source of funds.

Some believe that mortgage standards became lax because securitization gave rise to a form of moral hazard, whereby each link in the mortgage chain made a profit while passing any associated credit risk to the next link in the chain. At the same time, some financial firms retained significant amounts of the MBS they originated; thereby retaining significant amounts of credit risk and so were less guilty of moral hazard. Some argue this was not a flaw in the securitization concept *per se*, but in its implementation.

Inaccurate Credit Ratings

Credit rating agencies have given investment-grade ratings to CDOs and MBSs based on subprime mortgage loans. These high ratings were believed justified because of risk reducing practices, including over-collateralization, credit default insurance, and equity investors willing to bear the first losses. However, there are also indications that some involved in rating sub-prime-related securities knew at the time that the rating process was faulty as it was disclosed by emails exchanged between the employees of the credit rating agencies. These were later on disclosed by the government of USA.

High ratings encouraged investors to buy securities backed by subprime mortgages, helping finance the housing boom. The reliance on agency ratings and the way ratings were used to justify investments led many investors to treat securitized products—some based on subprime mortgages—as equivalent to higher quality securities.

Critics allege that the rating agencies suffered from conflicts of interest, as they were paid by investment banks and other firms that organize and sell structured securities to investors.

Government Policies

Both government action and inaction has contributed to the crisis. Some are of the opinion that the current American regulatory framework is outdated.

Increasing home ownership was a goal of the Clinton and Bush administrations. There is evidence that the Federal government leaned on the mortgage industry, including Fannie Mae and Freddie Mac (the GSE), to lower lending standards. Also, the U.S. Department of Housing and Urban Development's (HUD) mortgage policies fueled the trend towards issuing risky loans.

By 2008, the GSE owned, either directly or through mortgage pools they sponsored, $ 5.1 trillion in residential mortgages, about half the amount outstanding. The GSE have always been highly leveraged, their net worth as of 30 June 2008 being a mere US$ 114 billion. When concerns arose in September 2008 regarding the ability of the GSE to make good on their guarantees, the Federal government was forced to place the companies into a conservatorship, effectively nationalizing them at the taxpayers' expense.

Liberal economist Robert Kuttner has suggested that the repeal of the Glass-Steagall Act by the Gramm-Leach-Bliley Act of 1999 may have contributed to the subprime meltdown, but this is controversial. Economists have also debated the possible effects of the Community Reinvestment Act (CRA), with detractors claiming that the Act encouraged lending to uncreditworthy borrowers and defenders claiming a thirty year history of lending without increased risk.

Policies of Central Banks

Central banks manage monetary policy and may target the rate of inflation. They have some authority over commercial banks and possibly other financial institutions. They are less concerned with avoiding asset price bubbles, such as the housing bubble and dot-com bubble. Central banks have generally chosen to react after such bubbles burst so as to minimize collateral damage to the economy, rather than trying to prevent or stop the bubble itself. This is because identifying an asset bubble and determining the proper monetary policy to deflate it are matters of debate among economists.

Some market observers have been concerned that Federal Reserve actions could give rise to moral hazard. A Government Accountability Office critic said that the Federal Reserve Bank of New York's rescue of Long-Term Capital Management in 1998 would encourage large financial institutions to believe that the Federal Reserve would intervene on their behalf if risky loans went sour because they were "too big to fail."

A contributing factor to the rise in house prices was the Federal Reserve's lowering of interest rates early in the decade. From 2000 to 2003, the Federal Reserve lowered the federal funds rate target from 6.5% to 1.0%. This was done to soften the effects of the collapse of the dot-com bubble and of the September 2001 terrorist attacks, and to combat the perceived risk of deflation. The Fed believed that interest rates could be lowered safely primarily because the rate of inflation was low; it disregarded other important factors.

Financial Institution Debt Levels and Incentives

Many financial institutions, investment banks in particular, issued large amounts of debt during 2004-07, and invested the proceeds in mortgage-backed securities (MBS), essentially betting that house prices would continue to rise, and those households would continue to make their mortgage payments. Borrowing at a lower interest rate and investing the proceeds at a higher interest rate is a form of financial leverage. This is analogous to an individual taking out a second mortgage on his residence to invest in the stock market. This strategy proved profitable during the housing boom, but resulted in large losses when house prices began to decline and mortgages began to default. Beginning in 2007, financial institutions and individual investors holding MBS also suffered significant losses from mortgage payment defaults and the resulting decline in the value of MBS.

Three investment banks either went bankrupt (Lehman Brothers) or were sold at fire sale prices to other banks (Bear Stearns and Merrill Lynch) during September 2008. The failure of 3 of the 5 large USA investment banks augmented the instability in the global financial system. The remaining two investment banks, Morgan Stanley and Goldman Sachs, opted to become commercial banks, thereby subjecting themselves to more stringent regulation.

Credit Default Swaps

Credit defaults swaps (CDS) are financial instruments used as a hedge and protection for debt holders, in particular MBS investors, from the risk of default. As the net worth of banks and other financial institutions deteriorated because of losses related to sub-prime mortgages, the likelihood increased that those providing the insurance would have to pay their counterparties. This created uncertainty across the system, as investors wondered which companies would be required to pay to cover mortgage defaults.

Like all swaps and other financial derivatives, CDS may either be used to hedge risks or to profit from speculation. The volume of CDS outstanding increased 100-fold from 1998 to 2008, with estimates of the debt covered by CDS contracts, as of November 2008, ranging from US $ 33 to $ 47 trillion. CDS are lightly regulated. As of 2008, there was no central clearinghouse to honour CDS in the event a party to a CDS proved unable to perform his obligations under the CDS contract. Required disclosure of CDS-related obligations has been criticized as inadequate. Insurance companies such as American International Group (AIG), MBIA, and Ambac faced ratings downgrades because widespread mortgage defaults increased their potential exposure to CDS losses. These firms had to obtain additional funds (capital) to offset this exposure. AIG's having CDSs insuring $ 440 billion of MBS resulted in its seeking and obtaining a Federal government bailout.

Inflow of Funds Due to Trade Deficits

In 2005, Ben Bernanke addressed the implications of the USA's high and rising current account (trade) deficit, resulting from USA imports exceeding its exports. Between 1996 and 2004, the USA current account deficit increased by $ 650 billion, from 1.5% to 5.8% of GDP. Financing these deficits required the USA to borrow large sums from abroad, much of it from countries running trade surpluses, mainly the emerging economies in Asia and oil-exporting nations. The balance of payments identity requires that a country (such as the USA) running a current account deficit also have a capital account (investment) surplus of the same amount. Hence large and growing amounts of foreign funds (capital) flowed into the USA to finance its imports. Foreign investors had these funds to lend, either because they had very high personal savings rates (as high as 40% in China), or because of high oil prices. Bernanke referred to this as a "savings glut" that may have *pushed* capital into the USA, a view differing from that of mainstream economists, who view such capital as having been *pulled* into the USA by its high consumption levels. In other words, a nation cannot consume more than its income unless it sells assets to foreigners, or foreigners are willing to lend to it.

Regardless of the push or pull view, a "flood" of funds (capital or liquidity) reached the USA financial markets. Foreign governments supplied funds by purchasing USA Treasury bonds and thus avoided much of the direct impact of the crisis. USA households, on the other hand, used funds borrowed from foreigners to finance consumption or to bid up the prices of housing and financial assets. Financial institutions invested foreign funds in mortgage-backed securities.

IMPACT OF THE CRISIS

Impact in the U.S.

Between June 2007 and November 2008, Americans lost

more than a quarter of their net worth. By early November 2008, a broad U.S. stock index, the SandP 500, was down 45 percent from its 2007 high. Housing prices had dropped 20% from their 2006 peak, with futures markets signaling a 30-35% potential drop. Total home equity in the United States, which was valued at $ 13 trillion at its peak in 2006, had dropped to $ 8.8 trillion by mid-2008 and was still falling in late 2008. Total retirement assets, Americans' second-largest household asset, dropped by 22 percent, from $ 10.3 trillion in 2006 to $ 8 trillion in mid-2008. During the same period, savings and investment assets (apart from retirement savings) lost $ 1.2 trillion and pension assets lost $ 1.3 trillion. Taken together, these losses total a staggering $ 8.3 trillion.

Financial Market Impacts, 2007

The crisis began to affect the financial sector in February 2007, when HSBC, the world's largest (2008) bank, wrote down its holdings of subprime-related MBS by $ 10.5 billion, the first major subprime related loss to be reported during 2007, and at least 100 mortgage companies either shut down, suspended operations or were sold. Top management has not escaped unscathed, as the CEOs of Merrill Lynch and Citigroup resigned within a week of each other in late 2007. As the crisis deepened, more and more financial firms either merged, or announced that they were negotiating seeking merger partners.

During 2007, the crisis caused panic in financial markets and encouraged investors to take their money out of risky mortgage bonds and shaky equities and put it into commodities as "stores of value". Financial speculation in commodity futures following the collapse of the financial derivatives markets has contributed to the world food price crisis and oil price increases due to a "commodities super-cycle." Financial speculators seeking quick returns have removed trillions of dollars from equities and mortgage bonds, some of which has been invested into food and raw materials.

Mortgage defaults and provisions for future defaults caused profits at the 8533 USA depository institutions insured by the FDIC to decline from $ 35.2 billion in 2006 Q4 billion to $ 646 million in the same quarter a year later, a decline of 98%. 2007 Q4 saw the worst bank and thrift quarterly performance since 1990. In all of 2007, insured depository institutions earned approximately $ 100 billion, down 31% from a record profit of $ 145 billion in 2006. Profits declined from $ 35.6 billion in 2007 Q1 to $ 19.3 billion in 2008 Q1, a decline of 46%.

Financial Market Impacts, 2008

As of August 2008, financial firms around the globe have written down their holdings of subprime related securities by US$ 501 billion. The IMF estimates that financial institutions around the globe will eventually have to write off $ 1.5 trillion of their holdings of subprime MBSs. About $ 750 billion in such losses had been recognized as of November 2008. These losses have wiped out much of the capital of the world banking system.

When Lehman Brothers and other important financial institutions failed in September 2008, the crisis hit a key point. During a two day period in September 2008, $ 150 billion were withdrawn from USA money market funds. The average two day outflow had been $ 5 billion. The TED spreads, a measure of the risk of inter bank lending, quadrupled shortly after the Lehman failure. This credit freeze brought the global financial system to the brink of collapse. The response of the USA Federal Reserve, the European Central Bank, and other central banks was immediate and dramatic. During the last quarter of 2008, these central banks purchased US$ 2.5 trillion of government debt and troubled private assets from banks. This was the largest liquidity injection into the credit market, and the largest monetary policy action, in world history.

Indirect Economic Effects

The subprime crisis has had a number of adverse effects on the overall American economic situation. USA GDP was expected to contract at a 5.5% annual rate during Q4 2008. USA employers slashed 2.6 million jobs during 2008, the most since 1945. There have been significant job losses in the financial sector, with over 65,400 jobs lost in the USA as of September 2008. The unemployment rate climbed to 7.2% in December 2008, the highest level in 16 years.

Declining house prices have reduced household wealth and the collateral for home equity loans, which is placing downward pressure on consumption. The tightening of credit has caused a major decline in the sale of motor vehicles. Between October 2007 and October 2008, Ford sales were down 33.8%, General Motors sales were down 15.6%, and Toyota sales had declined 32.3%. Minorities have also born the brunt of the dramatic reduction in sub-prime lending. House-related crimes such as arson have increased. Many renters became innocent victims, by being evicted from their residences without notice, because their landlords' property has been foreclosed.

RESPONSES TO THE CRISIS

Various actions have been taken since the crisis became apparent in August 2007. In September 2008, major instability in world financial markets increased awareness and attention to the crisis. Various agencies and regulators, as well as political officials, began to take additional, more comprehensive steps to handle the crisis. To date, various government agencies have committed or spent trillions of dollars in loans, asset purchases, guarantees, and direct spending.

Legislative and Regulatory Responses

The central bank of the USA, the Federal Reserve, in partnership with central banks around the world, has taken several steps to address the crisis. Federal Reserve Chairman Ben Bernanke stated in early 2008: "Broadly, the Federal Reserve's response has followed two tracks: efforts to support market liquidity and functioning and the pursuit of our macroeconomic objectives through monetary policy." The Fed has:

- Lowered the target for the Federal funds rate from 5.25% to 2%, and the discount rate from 5.75% to 2.25%. This took place in six steps occurring between 18 September 2007 and 30 April 2008;
- Undertaken, along with other central banks, open market operations to ensure member banks remain liquid. These are effectively short-term loans to

member banks collateralized by government securities. Central banks have also lowered the interest rates (called the discount rate in the USA) they charge member banks for short-term loans;

- Used the Term Auction Facility (TAF) to provide short-term loans (liquidity) to banks. The Fed increased the monthly amount of these auctions throughout the crisis, raising it to $ 300 billion by November 2008, up from $ 20 billion at inception. A total of $ 1.6 trillion in loans to banks were made for various types of collateral by November 2008.
- Finalized, in July 2008, new rules for mortgage lenders;
- In October 2008, the Fed expanded the collateral it will lend against to include commercial paper, to help address continued liquidity concerns. By November 2008, the Fed had purchased $ 271 billion of such paper, out of a program limit of $ 1.4 trillion.
- In November 2008, the Fed announced the $ 200 billion Term Asset-Backed Securities Loan Facility (TALF). This program supported the issuance of asset-backed securities (ABS) collateralized by loans related to autos, credit cards, education, and small businesses. This step was taken to offset liquidity concerns.
- In November 2008, the Fed announced a $ 600 billion program to purchase the MBS of the GSE, to help lower mortgage rates.

Regulation

Regulators and legislators have contemplated taking action with respect to lending practices, bankruptcy protection, tax policies, affordable housing, credit counseling, education, and the licensing and qualifications of lenders. Regulations or guidelines can influence the transparency and reporting required of lenders and the types of loans they choose to issue. Congressional committees are also conducting hearings to help identify solutions and apply pressure to the various parties involved.

- On 31 March 2008, a sweeping expansion of the Fed's regulatory powers was proposed, that would expand its jurisdiction over non-bank financial institutions, and its authority to intervene in market crises.
- Responding to concerns that lending was not properly regulated, the House and Senate are both considering bills to further regulate lending practices.
- Countrywide's VIP program has led ethics experts and key senators to recommend that members of Congress be required to disclose information about the mortgages they take out.
- Non depository banks (e.g., investment banks and mortgage companies) are not subject to the same capital requirements as depository banks. Many investment banks had limited capital to offset declines in their holdings of MBSs, or to support their side of credit default insurance contracts.
- Nobel prize winner Joseph Stiglitz has recommended that the USA adopt regulations restricting leverage, and preventing companies from becoming "too big to fail."
- British Prime Minister Gordon Brown and Nobel laureate A. Michael Spence have argued for an "early warning system" to help detect a confluence of events leading to systemic risk. Dr. Ram Charan has also argued for risk management early warning systems at the corporate board level.
- On 18 September 2008, UK regulators announced a temporary ban on short-selling the stock of financial firms.
- The Australian government will invest AU$ 4 billion in mortgage backed securities issued by non-bank lenders, in an attempt to maintain competition in the mortgage market. However this is considered a drop in the ocean in regards to total lending.
- Fed Chairman Ben Bernanke stated there is a need for "well-defined procedures and authorities for dealing with the potential failure of a systemically important non-bank financial institution."

- Alan Greenspan has called for banks to have a 14% capital ratio, rather than the historical 8-10%. Major U.S. banks had capital ratios of around 12% in December 2008 after the initial round of bailout funds. The minimum capital ratio is regulated.
- Economists Nouriel Roubini and Lasse Pederson recommended in January 2009 that capital requirements for financial institutions be proportional to the systemic risk they pose, based on an assessment by regulators. Further, each financial institution would pay an insurance premium to the government based on its systemic risk.

Economic Stimulus Act of 2008

On 13 February 2008, President Bush signed into law an economic stimulus package costing $ 168 billion, mainly taking the form of income tax rebate checks mailed directly to taxpayers. Checks were mailed starting the week of 28 April 2008. However, this rebate coincided with an unexpected jump in gasoline and food prices. This coincidence led some to wonder whether the stimulus package would have the intended effect, or whether consumers would simply spend their rebates to cover higher food and fuel prices.

Housing and Economic Recovery Act of 2008

The Housing and Economic Recovery Act of 2008 included six separate major acts intended to restore confidence in the American mortgage industry. The Act were given as follows:

- Insures $ 300 billion in mortgages, that will assist an estimated 400,000 borrowers;
- Creates a new Federal regulator to ensure the safe and sound operation of the GSEs (Fannie Mae and Freddie Mac) and Federal Home Loan Banks;
- Raises the ceiling on the dollar value of the mortgages the government sponsored enterprises (GSEs) may purchase;
- Lends money to mortgage bankers to help them refinance the mortgages of owner-occupants at risk

of foreclosure. The lender reduces the amount of the mortgage (typically taking a significant loss), in exchange for sharing in any future appreciation in the selling price of the house via the Federal Housing Administration. The refinancing must have fixed payments for a term of 30 years;

- Requires that lenders disclose more information about the products they offer and the deals they close; and
- Helps local governments buy and renovate foreclosed properties.

Failures and Government Bailouts of Financial Firms

The failures and government bailouts of financial firms are described in detail in the following paragraphs:

- Northern Rock, encountering difficulty obtaining the credit it required to remain in business, was nationalized on 17 February 2008. As of October 8, 2008, United Kingdom taxpayer liability arising from this takeover had risen to £87 billion ($ 150 billion).
- Bear Stearns was acquired by J.P. Morgan Chase in March 2008 for $ 1.2 billion. The sale was conditional on the Fed's lending Bear Sterns US$ 29 billion on a non recourse basis.
- IndyMac Bank, America's leading Alt-A originator in 2006 with approximately $ 32 billion in deposits was placed into conservatorship by the FDIC on July 11, 2008, citing liquidity concerns. A bridge bank, IndyMac Federal Bank, FSB, was established under the control of the FDIC.
- The GSEs Fannie Mae and Freddie Mac were both placed in conservatorship in September 2008. The two GSE's guarantee or hold mortgage backed securities (MBS), mortgages and other debt with a Notional value of more than $ 5 trillion.
- Merrill Lynch was acquired by Bank of America in September 2008 for $ 50 billion.
- Scottish banking group HBOS agreed on 17 September 2008 to an emergency acquisition by its

UK rival Lloyds TSB, after a major decline in HBOS's share price stemming from growing fears about its exposure to British and American MBSs. The UK government made this takeover possible by agreeing to waive its competition rules.

- Lehman Brothers declared bankruptcy on 15 September 2008, after the Secretary of the Treasury Henry Paulson, citing moral hazard, refused to bail it out.
- AIG received an $ 85 billion emergency loan in September 2008 from the Federal Reserve which AIG is expected to repay by gradually selling-off its assets. In exchange, the Federal government acquired a 79.9% equity stake in AIG.
- Washington Mutual (WaMu) was seized in September 2008 by the USA Office of Thrift Supervision (OTS). Most of WaMu's untroubled assets were to be sold to J.P. Morgan Chase.
- British bank Bradford and Bingley was nationalised on 29 September 2008 by the UK government. The government assumed control of the bank's £50 billion mortgage and loan portfolio, while its deposit and branch network are to be sold to Spain's Grupo Santander.
- In October 2008, the Australian government announced that it would make AU$ 4 billion available to non-bank lenders unable to issue new loans. After discussion with the industry, this amount was increased to AU$ 8 billion.
- In November 2008, the U.S. government announced it was purchasing $ 27 billion of preferred stock in Citigroup, a USA bank with over $ 2 trillion in assets, and warrants on 4.5% of its common stock. The preferred stock carries an 8% dividend. This purchase follows an earlier purchase of $ 25 billion of the same preferred stock using TARP funds.

Emergency Economic Stabilization Act of 2008

On 19 September 2008, the U.S. Federal government announced a plan, requiring Congressional approval, to purchase from financial institutions large amounts of mortgage backed securities (MBSs) and collateralized debt obligation (CDOs) backed by subprime mortgages. The estimated cost of this plan was at least $ 700 billion. The plan also banned short-selling the stocks of financial firms. On 29 September 2008, the House of Representatives rejected a revised version of the plan. On 1 October, 2008, the U.S. Senate approved an amended version of the plan, which was ratified by the House on October 3 and immediately signed into law by President Bush. After the law was passed, the U.S. Treasury instead primarily used the first $ 350 billion of bailout funds to buy preferred stock in banks instead of troubled mortgage assets.

Lending Industry Action

Both lenders and borrowers may benefit from avoiding foreclosure, which is a costly and lengthy process. Some lenders have offered troubled borrowers more favorable mortgage terms (i.e., refinancing, loan modification or loss mitigation). Borrowers have also been encouraged to contact their lenders to discuss alternatives. Corporations, trade groups, and consumer advocates have begun to cite data on the numbers and types of borrowers assisted by loan modification programs. A report in January 2008 stated that mortgage lenders modified 54,000 loans and established 183,000 repayment plans in the third quarter of 2007, a period in which there were 384,000 foreclosures were initiated.

In December 2008, the U.S. FDIC reported that more than half of mortgages modified during the first half of 2008 were delinquent again, in many cases because payments were not reduced or mortgage debt was not forgiven.

On October 5, 2008, the Bank of America, following on a legal settlement with several states, announced a more aggressive and systematic program intended to help an estimated 400,000 borrowers keep their homes. The program will limit payments as a fraction of household income, and reduce mortgage balances.

In November 2008, Fannie Mae, Freddie Mac and their network of mortgage service providers announced a streamlined loan modification program and foreclosure suspension, designed to help keep borrowers in their homes.

Several Australian lenders have amended their policies for higher risk mortgage types. These changes have been relatively minor, with the exception of those nonconforming lenders that lend to credit impaired and sub-prime borrowers. It remains to be seen if this trend will continue, or if Australian lenders will eventually stop offering riskier loan products.

Hope Now Alliance

President George W. Bush announced a plan to voluntarily and temporarily freeze the mortgages of a limited number of mortgage debtors holding ARMs. A refinancing facility called FHA-Secure was also created. These actions are part of the Hope Now Alliance, an ongoing collaborative effort between the US Government and private industry to help certain sub-prime borrowers. In February 2008, the Alliance reported that during the second half of 2007, it had helped 545,000 sub-prime borrowers with shaky credit, or 7.7% of 7.1 million sub-prime loans outstanding as of September 2007.

During February 2008, a program called "Project Lifeline" was announced. Six of the largest USA lenders, in partnership with the Hope Now Alliance, agreed to defer foreclosure actions for 30 days for borrowers 90 or more days delinquent on their mortgage payments. The intent of the program was to reduce foreclosures by encouraging loan adjustments.

Bank Capital Replenishment from Private Sources

As of May 2008, major financial institutions had obtained over $ 260 billion in new capital, taking the form of bonds or preferred stock sold to private investors in exchange for cash. This new capital has helped banks maintain required capital ratios, which have declined significantly due to losses on sub-prime loans or CDO investments. Raising additional capital has been advocated by the leadership of the U.S. Federal Reserve and the Treasury Department. Well-capitalized banks are in a better position to lend at favourable interest rates, and to offset the falling liquidity and rising uncertainty in credit markets. Banks have obtained some of their new capital from the sovereign wealth funds of developing countries, which may have political implications. Certain major banks and 666 financial institutions have also reduced their dividend payouts to stabilize their financial position. Steven Pearlstein has advocated government guarantees for new preferred stock, to encourage investors to provide private capital to the banks.

Litigation

Litigation related to the subprime crisis is underway. A study released in February 2008 indicated that 278 civil lawsuits were filed in federal courts during 2007 related to the subprime crisis. The number of filings in state courts was not quantified but is also believed to be significant. The study found that 43% of the cases were class actions brought by borrowers, such as those that contended they were victims of discriminatory lending practices. Other cases include securities lawsuits filed by investors, commercial contract disputes, employment class actions, and bankruptcy-related cases. Defendants included mortgage bankers, brokers, lenders, appraisers, title companies, home builders, servicer, issuers, underwriters, bond insurers, money managers, public accounting firms, and company boards and officers.

Law Enforcement

The number of Federal Bureau of Investigation (FBI) agents assigned to mortgage-related crimes increased by 50% between 2007 and 2008. In June 2008, the FBI stated that its mortgage fraud caseload has doubled in the past three years to more than 1,400 pending cases. Between 1 March and 18 June 2008, 406 people were arrested for mortgage fraud in an FBI sting across the country. People arrested include buyers, sellers and others across the wide-ranging mortgage industry. On 8 March 2008, the FBI began a probe of Countrywide for possible fraudulent lending practices, securities fraud.

Ethics Investigation

On 18 June 2008, a Congressional ethics panel started examining allegations that Democrat Senators Christopher Dodd of Connecticut (the sponsor of a major $ 300 billion housing rescue bill) and Kent Conrad of North Dakota received preferential loans by troubled mortgage lender Countrywide Financial Corp.

Executive Compensation Reform

Banks and executives are under pressure to reduce bonuses, as much of the profits recognized by major banks were wiped out by subsequent losses during the crisis. The extent of risk taken was not properly factored into bonus computations. Several executives have foregone bonuses in light of what turned out to be poor performance. Credit Suisse bank announced it will begin paying bonuses out of a fund containing troubled assets on its books, in place of cash. Gains or losses on the fund will affect employee bonuses. This approach was praised as "monstrously clever" by one analyst.

EFFECT ON FINANCIAL CONDITION OF US GOVERNMENT UNITS

The Federal government's efforts to support the global financial system have resulted in significant new financial commitments, totaling $ 7 trillion by November, 2008. These commitments can be characterized as investments, loans, and loan guarantees, rather than direct expenditures. In many cases, the government purchased financial assets such as commercial paper, mortgage-backed securities, or other types of asset-backed paper, to enhance liquidity in frozen markets. As the crisis has progressed, the Fed has expanded the collateral against which it is willing to lend to include higher-risk assets.

The extent to which the Federal government is at risk because of these investments and guarantees remains to be seen. The upshot has been a US $ 1 trillion increase in the national debt of the USA during FY 2008, compared to an average increase of US$ 550 billion during the previous five years. The total debt reached $ 10 trillion in September 2008.

In addition, state and local government property tax collections are expected to decline because of an estimated $ 1.2 trillion reduction in housing prices, and a slowing of the overall American economy. This expectation is affecting the ability of state governments to finance their operations through bond sales. Finding themselves unable to borrow, the states of California and Massachusetts have requested that the Fed lend them the amounts they would have borrowed elsewhere under normal conditions.

Stifel Nicolaus, writing in Market Watch, has claimed that the problem mortgages are not confined to the subprime niche: "the rapidly increasing scope and depth of the problems in the mortgage market suggest that the entire sector has plunged into a downward spiral similar to the subprime woes whereby each negative development feeds further deterioration," calling it a "vicious cycle" and adding that lenders "continue to believe conditions will get worse".

On 19 May, 2008, Nouriel Roubini, a professor at New York University and head of Roubini Global Economics, was quoted as saying that if the economy slips into recession "then you have a systemic banking crisis like we haven't had since the 1930s".

Because debt instruments backed by subprime mortgages were purchased worldwide, the International Monetary Fund (IMF) "says that worldwide losses stemming from the USA subprime mortgage crisis could run to $ 945 billion."

As of February 2009, analysts were predicting that Alt-A loans, offered to those with good credit but less steady income than prime borrowers, represent the next wave of delinquencies and foreclosures. Rating agency Moody's expects the delinquency rate to increase to over 20%, compared with the historical average of below 1%. Analysts at Goldman Sachs estimate write-downs on the $ 1.3 trillion of total Alt-A debt at $ 600 billion, almost as much as expected sub-prime losses. Add in option ARMs, many of which are essentially the same as Alt-A, and the potential impact climbs towards $ 1 trillion.

Francis Fukuyama has argued that the crisis represents the end of Reaganism in the financial sector, which was characterized by lighter regulation, pared-back government, and lower taxes. Significant financial sector regulatory changes are expected as a result of the crisis.

Fareed Zakaria believes that the crisis may force Americans and their government to live within their means. Further, some of the best minds may be redeployed from financial engineering to more valuable business activities, or to science and technology.

Roger Altman wrote that "the crash of 2008 has inflicted profound damage on [the U.S.] financial system, its economy, and its standing in the world; the crisis is an important geopolitical setback...the crisis has coincided with historical forces that were already shifting the world's focus away from the United States. Over the medium term, the United States will have to operate from a smaller global platform—while others, especially China, will have a chance to rise faster."

The crisis has cast doubt on the legacy of Alan Greenspan, the Chairman of the Federal Reserve System from 1986 to January 2006. Senator Chris Dodd claimed that Greenspan created the "perfect storm" Greenspan has remarked that there is a one-in-three chance of recession from the fallout. When asked to comment on the crisis, Greenspan spoke as follows:

The current credit crisis will come to an end when the overhang of inventories of newly built homes is largely liquidated, and home price deflation comes to an end. That will stabilize the now-uncertain value of the home equity that acts as a buffer for all home mortgages, but most importantly for those held as collateral for residential mortgage-backed securities. Very large losses will, no doubt, be taken as a consequence of the crisis. But after a period of protracted adjustment, the U.S. economy, and the world economy more generally, will be able to get back to business.

A culture of consumerism is a factor "in an economy based on immediate gratification." Economist Nouriel Roubini wrote in January 2009 that sub-prime mortgage defaults triggered the broader global credit crisis, but were just one symptom of multiple debt bubble collapses: "This crisis is not merely the result of the U.S. housing bubble's bursting or the collapse of the United States' subprime mortgage sector. The credit excesses that created this disaster were global. There were many bubbles, and they extended beyond housing in many countries to commercial real estate mortgages and loans, to credit cards, auto loans, and student loans. There were bubbles for the securitized products that converted these loans and mortgages into complex, toxic, and destructive financial instruments. And there were still more bubbles for local government borrowing, leveraged buyouts, hedge funds, commercial and industrial loans, corporate bonds, commodities, and credit-default swaps..." It is the bursting of the many bubbles that he believes is causing this crisis to spread globally and magnify its impact.

CONCLUSION

At last, it can be concluded from the above discussion that like any other crisis, the sub-prime crisis is also the result of some of the mistakes made by the human being. These mistakes, needless to say are the result of greed of the mankind. So this crisis also gives a lesson that if any decision is based on the greed and not on the fundamentals, and then it is going to trouble the mankind.

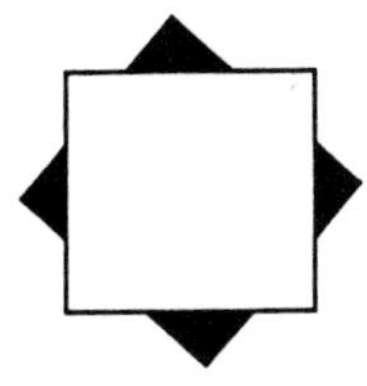

Bibliography

Akbar, E.T. (2008), "Global Financial Meltdown and the Demise of Neoliberalism" at http://www.globalresearch.ca/index.php?context=va&aid=10549 retrieved on 15-10-2008 at 1230 hrs.

Alan, G. (2007), The Age of Turbulence, The Penguin Press.

Andrews, E.L. (2008), "Vast Bailout by U.S. Proposed in Bid to Stem Financial Crisis", *The New York Times,* September 18.

Anonymous (2008), "SEC Proposes Comprehensive Reforms to Bring Increased Transparency to Credit Rating Process", U.S. Securities and Exchange Commission. 2008, available at http://www.sec.gov/news/press/2008/2008-110.htm, retrieved on July 2008.

Anonymous (2008), "The Fed Bails out AIG", *Business Week* at http://www.businessweek.com/bwdaily/dnflash/content/sep2008/db20080916_387203.htm?chan=top+news_top+news+index+-+temp_top+story, retrieved on 17 September 2008.

Aversa, J. (2008), "Rebate Checks in the Mail by Spring", *The Huffington Post,* http://www.huffingtonpost.com/2008/02/13/rebate-checks-in-the-mail_n_86525.html, retrieved on 19 May 2008

Bajaj, V. (2008), "Stocks Are Hurt by Latest Fear: Declining Prices", *New York Times,* November 20.

Banco de México, The Mexican Economy, 1996: Financial Assistance Package, Annual Report.

Banerjee (1992), 'A simple model of herd behavior', *Quarterly Journal of Economics*, Volume 107, Issue 3, pp. 797-817.

Ben, S.B. (1983). "Non-Monetary Effects of the Financial Crisis in the Propagation of the Great Depression", *The American Economic Review*, Volume 73, Issue 3, pp. 257–76.

———, (2008), "Mortgage Delinquencies and Foreclosures", Columbia Business School's 32nd Annual Dinner, New York, New York (2008-05-05)

———, (2008), "Statement by Federal Reserve Board Chairman Ben S. Bernanke", Board of Governors of the Federal Reserve System available at http://www.federalreserve.gov/newsevents/press/other/20080907a.htm, retrieved on 10 September 2008.

Benjamin, D., "Occupy, Resist, Produce: Worker Cooperatives in Argentina" at http://upsidedownworld.org/coops_arg.htm

Bootle, R. (2008), "Pound fall is UK's get-out-of-jail-free card", *The Daily Telegraph* at http://www.telegraph.co.uk/money/main.jhtml?xml=/money/2008/04/28/ccom128.xml

Brent, D.G., David, K. and David, A.M. (2006), "Was There Too Little Entry During the Dot Com Era?" Robert H. Smith School Research Paper No. RHS 06-029 Available at SSRN: http://ssrn.com/abstract=899100

Carney, R., (2009), Lessons from the Asian Financial Crisis, New York, NY: Routledge

Chari, V. and Kehoe, P. (2004), 'Financial Crises as Herds: Overturning the Critiques', *Journal of Economic Theory*, Volume 119, pp. 128-50.

Charles, P.K. and Robert, A. (2005), Manias, Panics, and Crashes: A History of Financial Crises, 5th edition, Wiley.

Cheetham, R. (1998), Asia Crisis. Paper presented at conference, U.S.-ASEAN-Japan Policy Dialogue, School of Advanced International Studies of Johns Hopkins University, June 7-9, Washingtion, D.C.

Christina, D.R. (1992), "What Ended the Great Depression", *Journal of Economic History*, Volume 52, No. 4, pp. 757-784

Colin, R. (2009), Global Financial Meltdown: How we can Avoid the Next Economic Crisis, New York, Palgrave Macmillan

Craig, B., Martin, E. and Sergio, R. (2008), 'Currency crisis models', *New Palgrave Dictionary of Economics*, 2nd edition.

D. Diamond and Dybvig, P. (1983), 'Bank runs, deposit insurance, and liquidity', *Journal of Political Economy*, Volume 91, Issue 3, pp. 401-19.

Darryl McLeod (2002), 'Capital Flight', in the Concise Encyclopedia of Economics at the Library of Economics and Liberty.

David, L. (1999), Thailand's Scapegoat? Battling Extradition Over Charges of Embezzlement, a Financier Says he's the fall guy for the 1997 Financial Crash, TIME.com. 27 December

Demyanyk, Y. and Hemert, O.V. (2008), "Understanding the Subprime Mortgage Crisis", Working Paper Series, Social Science Electronic Publishing at http://papers.ssrn.com/sol3/papers.cfm?abstract_id=1020396. Retrieved on 18-09-2008.

Desai, P. (2000), Why Did the Ruble Collapse in August 1998?, *The American Economic Review*, Vol. 90, No. 2, pp. 58-66.

Duhigg, C. (2008), "Depression, You Say? Check Those Safety Nets", *New York Times*, March 23.

Editorial (1998), the IMF Crisis, *Wall Street Journal*, 15 April

Eric, W. (2007), "Subprime Bailout: Good Idea or 'Moral Hazard" at http://www.npr.org/templates/story/story.php?storyId=16734629, retrieved on 29-11-2007.

Fisher, R.W. (2006), "Confessions of a Data Dependent: Remarks before the New York Association for Business Economics" available at http://dallasfed.org/news/speeches/fisher/2006/fs061102.cfm, retrieved on 13-07-2008

Fletcher, T.W. (1961), "The Great Depression of English Agriculture 1873-96", *The Economic History Review*, Volume 13, No. 3, pp. 417-32

Fotopoulos, T. (2008), "The Myths about the Economic Crisis, the Reformist Left and Economic Democracy", *The International Journal of Inclusive Democracy,* Volume 4, No. 4, pp. 56-67.

Fredric, M. (1978), "The Household Balance and the Great Depression", *Journal of Economic History,* Volume 38, pp. 918–37.

Friedman, M. and Schwartz, A. (1971), A Monetary History of the United States, 1867-1960. Princeton University Press.

Gaidar, Y. (1999), Lessons of the Russian Crisis for Transition Economies, *Finance and Development,* Vol. 36, No. 2, pp. 76-85.

Garber, P. (2001), Famous First Bubbles: The Fundamentals of Early Manias, MIT Press.

George, S. (2008), The New Paradigm for Financial Markets—The Credit Crisis of 2008 and what it Means, New York: Public Affairs.

Gretchen, M. (2008), "The Reckoning: How the Thundering Herd Faltered and Fell". *New York Times* at http://www.nytimes.com/2008/11/09/business/09magic.html, retrieved on 13 November 2008.

Henry, B. and Nixon, J. (1998), "The Crisis in Russia: Some Initial Observations", *Economic Outlook,* Vol. 23, No. 1, pp. 38-46.

Herszenhorn, D.M. (2008), "$700 Billion Is Sought for Wall Street in Vast Bailout", *The New York Times,* September 20.

Holden, L. (2007), "Moral hazard' helps shape mortgage mess" at http://www.bankrate.com/brm/news/mortgages/20070418_subprime_mortgage_morality_a1.asp?caret=3c.

Howard, H. (2000), "The Trillion-Dollar Bank Shakedown That Bodes Ill for Cities", *City Journal.* http://www.city-journal.org/html/10_1_the_trillion_dollar.html, accessed on 01-01-2000.

http://en.wikipedia.org

http://en.wikipedia.org/wiki/1994_economic_crisis_in_Mexico, retrieved on 15-01-2009 at 1000 hrs.

http://en.wikipedia.org/wiki/Japanese_asset_price_bubble retrieved on 16-01-2009 at 1245 hrs.

http://en.wikipedia.org/wiki/Japanese_asset_price_bubble, retrieved on 16-01-2009 at 1130 hrs.

http://en.wikipedia.org/wiki/Latin_American_debt_crisis, retrieved on 15-01-2009 at 1030 hrs.

http://papers.ssrn.com

Hunnicutt, S. (2009), The American housing crisis, Farmington Hills, MI: Green Haven Press.

Irving, F. (1933), "The Debt-Deflation Theory of Great Depressions", *Econometrica*, Volume 1, pp. 337-57.

James, P., Guha, K., Dombey, D. and Morris, H. (2008), "Central banks pump cash into system", *The Financial Times* at http://www.ft.com/cms/s/0/f9525dd4-8d24-11dd-83d5-0000779fd18c.html, retrieved on 29 September 2008.

John, P.H. (2008), "Credit Rating Agencies and the 'Worldwide Credit Crisis': The Limits of Reputation, the Insufficiency of Reform, and a Proposal for Improvement" at http://www.law.berkeley.edu/files/RAShortWhitePaper JH090908KTrev-1.pdf. retrieved on 05-09-2008

Jon, B. (2008), "Will foreclosures spark an arson boom?", http://money.cnn.com/2008/01/09/news/economy/birger_arson.fortune/, accessed on 09-01-2008

Jutta, M. (2006), Hyperinflation, Currency Board, and Bust: The Case of Argentina, Peter Lang Publishing; 1st edition

Kahn D.S., (2008), 'A systemic crisis demands systemic solutions', *The Financial Times*, Sept. 25, 2008.

Kaufman, G. and Scott, K. (2003),'What is Systemic Risk, and do Bank Regulators Retard or Contribute to it?' *The Independent Review*, Volume 7, Issue 3, pp. 45-56.

Kaufman, G.G., Krueger, T.H., Hunter, W.C. (1999), The Asian Financial Crisis: Origins, Implications and Solutions, Springer.

Kim, L. (September 2008), "Lehman tumbles, Merrill Lynch totters on Meltdown Monday", ABC News, at http://www.abc.net.au/news/stories/2008/09/16/2365548.htm, retrieved on 17 September 2008.

Krugman, P. (1979), 'A Model of Balance-of-payments Crises', *Journal of Money*, Credit and Banking, Volume 11, pp. 311-25.

Laeven, L. and Valencia, F. (2008), 'Systemic banking crises: a new database', International Monetary Fund Working Paper 08/224.

Lahart, J. (2007). "Egg Cracks Differ In Housing, Finance Shells". WSJ.com (Wall Street Journal) at http://online.wsj.com/article/SB119845906460548071.html?mod=googlenews_wsj. Retrieved on 13 July 2008.

Lawrence, W.J. (1991), The S&L Debacle: Public Policy Lessons for Bank and Thrift Regulation, New York: Oxford University Press

Les, C. (2008), "No help for 70% of subprime borrowers" at http://money.cnn.com/2008/04/22/real_estate/no_help_for_most_borrowers/index.htm?cnn=yes, retrieved on 17 September 2008.

Liebowitz, S. (2009) "Anatomy of a Train Wreck: Causes of the Mortgage Meltdown" in Randall Holcombe and B.W. Powell, (eds.), Housing America: Building out of a Crisis, Oakland CA: The Independent Institute.

Louis, U. (1996). "H.P. Minsky, 77, Economist Who Decoded Lending Trends", *New York Times*, October 26.

Lowy, M. (1991), High Rollers: Inside the Savings and Loan Debacle. New York: Praeger

Mark, C.K. (2003), How Governments Privatize: The Politics of Divestment in the United States and Germany, Washington: Georgetown University Press.

Martin, F. (2008), "Trouble Without Borders". *The New York Times* available at http://www.nytimes.com/2008/10/24/business/worldbusiness/24won.html, retrieved on 24 October 2008.

Martin, M. (1992), The Greatest Ever Bank Robbery: The Collapse of the Savings and Loan Industry, New York: C. Scribner's Sons.

Michael, A.R. (1990), Overdrawn: The Bailout of American Savings, New York: Dutton.

Michael, H. and Dennis, N. (2008), "Heavy stock losses after Fed action", *The Financial Times* at http://www.ft.com/cms/s/0/d925b966-8dec-11dd-8089-0000779fd18c.html, retrieved on 29 September 2008.

Michael, L. (1991), High Rollers: Inside the Savings and Loan Debacle, New York: Praeger.

Michael, M.G. and Jolly, D. (2008), "It's Official: Recession Started One Year Ago", *The New York Times*. http://www.nytimes.com/2008/12/02/business/02markets.html, retrieved on 1 December 2008.

Mike, D. (2004), 21 Dog Years, Free Press.

Noland, Markus, Li-gang Liu, Sherman Robinson, and Zhi Wang, (1998) Global Economic Effects of the Asian Currency Devaluations, Policy Analyses in International Economics, No. 56, Washington, DC, Institute for International Economics.

Obstfeld, M. (1996), 'Models of currency crises with self-fulfilling features'. *European Economic Review*, Volume 40, Issue 3, pp. 1037-47.

Paul, B. (2001), The Chastening: Inside the Crisis that Rocked the Global Financial System and Humbled the IMF, Public Affairs

Pempel, T.J. (1999), The Politics of the Asian Economic Crisis, Ithaca, NY: Cornell University Press.

Pinto, B., Gurvich, E. and Ulatov, S. (2004), Lessons from the Russian Crisis of 1998 and Recovery, The World Bank Report.

Richard, H. (1998), China's Decisive Role in the Asian Financial Crisis, Global Beat Issue Brief No. 24, 27 January

Roger, B. (2008), "Pound fall is UK's get-out-of-jail-free card", *The Daily Telegraph*, at http://www.telegraph.co.uk/money/main.jhtml?xml=/money/2008/04/28/ccom128.xml.

Roger, L. (2004), Origins of the Crash: The Great Bubble and Its Undoing, Penguin Books.

Schlesinger, Jr., Arthur M. (2003), The Coming of the New Deal: 1933-1935, Paperback ed. New York: Houghton Mifflin.

Shigenori Shiratsuka (2003), Asset Price Bubble in Japan in the 1980s: Lessons for Financial and Macroeconomic Stability, Discussion Paper No. 2003-E-15, Bank of Japan Whitepaper accessed at http://www.imes.boj.or.jp/english/publication/edps/2003/03-E-15.pdfPDF, retrieved on 20-01-2009 at 1230 hrs.

Steven, P., Mary, F., Paul, M. (1989), Inside Job: The Looting of America's Savings and Loans, New York: McGraw-Hill.

Stiglitz, J. (1996), Some Lessons from the East Asian Miracle, the World Bank Research Observer.

The Mexican Economy 1996: Financial Assistance Package—Annual Report of the Banco de México.

The World Fact book, 2006.

Tiwari, R. (2003), Post-crisis Exchange Rate Regimes in Southeast Asia, Seminar Paper, University of Hamburg.

Vasiliev, S.A., (2000), Overview of Structural Reforms in Russia after 1998 Financial Crisis, A Report by International Monetary Fund.

Wilder, R. (2008), "Why Exactly does the Fed Pay Interest on Reserves?" RGE Monitor (Roubini Global Economics, LLC)

William, B.K. (2005), The Best Way to Rob a Bank is to Own One. Austin: University of Texas Press.

Yellen, J.L. (2007), The Asian Financial Crisis Ten Years Later: Assessing the Past and Looking to the Future, Speech to the Asia Society of Southern California, Los Angeles, California, 6 February 2007.

Index